Birmingham City Transport

Malcolm Keeley

Ian Allan PUBLISHING

Front cover:
End of the line — the very last of the traditional Birmingham half-cabs to be built. Bus 3227 comprised a Daimler CVG6 chassis and 55-seat bodywork by Crossley, and entered service on 1 October 1954. It is seen in Baldwins Lane, Hall Green, just one stop away from the terminus of service 91, in May 1969. *Malcolm Keeley*

Back cover:
Birmingham City Transport was famous for its vague destinations. Radial services showed the outer terminus even when the buses were city-bound; the bus stop plate would show the direction of travel. Hall Green residents would not have made much of the description WELLHEAD LANE, a comparatively insignificant thoroughfare on the other side of the city that happened to be the home of Perry Barr garage. 1950 Park Royal-bodied Leyland Titan PD2 2224 is passing beneath the bridge carrying the Birmingham-Stratford railway line over Robin Hood Lane, returning to Perry Barr in June 1969 after working the Pheasey-Hall Green cross-city service 90/91; the bus being on loan from Yardley Wood garage. *Malcolm Keeley*

Title page:
The first impression of Birmingham received by visitors on most main roads was presented by an immaculate corporation bus turning at the boundary due to the 1914 agreement with Midland Red. 1939 Metro-Cammell-bodied Daimler COG5 1231 is seen at the Maypole in August 1949. The huge roadside public house of that name may have gone but the Maypole is still visited by BCT buses, even a COG5, thanks to supporters of The Transport Museum, Wythall, which is nearby. *John Edgington*

First published 2007

ISBN (10) 0 7110 3167 3
ISBN (13) 978 0 7110 3167 8

Published by Ian Allan Publishing

an imprint of Ian Allan Publishing Ltd, Hersham, Surrey KT12 4RG.
Printed in England by Ian Allan Printing Ltd, Hersham, Surrey KT12 4RG.

Code: 0704/B1

Visit the Ian Allan Publishing website at www.ianallanpublishing.com

CONTENTS

Bibliography

Those wishing to read further are recommended to look out for 'Birmingham City Transport', published by TPC in 1978 and now hard to find. For fuller detail, you are recommended David Harvey's generously illustrated series of books on Birmingham's tramways, trolleybuses and motorbuses, published by Silver Link Publishing. The ultimate detailed works on BCT motorbuses are the PSV Circle publications 'PD9' and 'PD10', published in 1967/8. All these were of great help in writing this book.

Malcolm Keeley
Shirley, Solihull
January 2007

INTRODUCTION

What a treat to be able to describe an organisation for which the glory days did not decline into a morass. BCT was struggling for platform staff but, in most respects, it was weathering the misfortunes besetting other operators when Labour politicians snuffed it out in 1969. Its buses, like everything about BCT, were well-specified and well-maintained. It ran like a well-oiled machine, much like the British Army from which so many of its personnel had been drawn.

As children in the late 1950s, sneaking into any BCT garage was a daunting experience. Garage traffic supervisors were all cast from the same mould — ex-Army of course, immaculate, not necessarily tall but heavily built, penetrating eyes designed to look through the toughest conductor and deter any idea of argument. Drivers and conductors turned the proverbial blind eye provided you looked harmless but there was the particular fear of running across 'the man in the white coat' — the senior engineer who protected 'his' buses with commendable ferocity and was in no way approachable! There were, of course, fitters who invited you to sit in the driver's cab and encouraged your interest in buses; sadly today such kindly acts are surrounded by all manner of safety and child protection issues, to the loss of our pastime. BCT organised enthusiasts in an appropriately military manner with a different garage being made available for our inspection on a Sunday morning. Every visit encouraged the fascination of BCT — its quality and efficiency — not perfect, of course, but close! I joined Birmingham City Transport in 1965 and clearly recall the sad day in 1969 when we began to answer the phone with the dreadful name West Midlands Passenger Transport Executive plus your departmental identification!

This book concentrates on the years after 1937 when the undertaking became known as Birmingham City Transport, deleting the word Tramways from its title and dedicating itself to a motorbus future. I loved BCT's buses, and still do, especially the exposed-radiator ones. You will not find

this author following the widespread use by other enthusiasts in recent times of the term 'BCT Standards', meaning the 'New Look' buses. BCT did indeed refer to 'Standard' buses, but these were *any* double-deckers that were not the new, large-capacity Daimler Fleetlines and Leyland Atlanteans. BCT buses are still about in preservation and I am pleased to have played a part in that. Virtually every owner of an ex-BCT bus is marked by a preparedness to invest lots of hard cash and many hours to ensure the result perpetuates the BCT philosophy of excellence.

I must thank all those kind photographers who have contributed to this book, particularly the colour contributors whose slides, of course, do not have a

▲ The Corporation's first buses were 10 Daimler CC models with 34-seat bodies by London General; the three here are about to be delivered in 1913. The chassis were taken by the War Department in 1914, following the outbreak of World War I. The bodies were refitted to new Tilling-Stevens TS3 chassis, a type exempted by the War Department which did not favour its petrol-electric transmission. *MRK Collection*

negative. Graham Stone astonished me by coolly producing a picture of bus 1327. Thanks also to Bob Deloyde for his help on one particularly choice picture. The book prompted several entertaining letters from R. A. (Bob) Mills who was extremely active in the first ten years after World War 2, photographing BCT's bus developments and catching many of the rarities. His work has graced BCT books over the years; without his efforts we would be much poorer.

I also pay a particular tribute to a largely unsung hero, Mr F. W. York. Many of Fred's pictures have been published but very often under the names of others, who have been in possession of his negatives. It was Fred, however, who set out 50 years ago to record the buses and changing streets of Birmingham. This was a well-timed quest because it coincided with the brief return of prewar Daimler COG5s to the roads in the late 1950s and was just in time to record Brum before and during the rebuilding of the city and inner areas.

Having access to many hundreds of Fred's negatives, I can confirm that he was out in all weathers, often on foot, including complete circuits of the Inner Circle route. Without his work, the record of Birmingham's buses would be much diminished.

My search to fill gaps in my understanding of BCT

engineering logic led to some enjoyable correspondence with a transport hero of mine, Alan Townsin, and a morning of hilarious reminiscences, mostly unpublishable, with the legendary Larry Locke, BCT's Test Engineer. I also thank my old friend Monty Russell, who has generously shared his notes with me over several decades and kindly looked over the manuscript. He would no doubt join me in thanking in turn other researchers of Birmingham's transport history, especially the late Peter Hardy who encouraged our interest. Much of this information is now with the Kithead Trust where trustees Peter Jaques and Derek Potter gave me every assistance. Thanks too to Phil Drake who donated the extensive notes by his father, Derek V. Drake to The Transport Museum, Wythall. Moving back to pictures, Terry Walsh was frequently consigned to his darkroom to get the best out of negatives. Finally thanks to my regular partner in grime, Paul Gray, for his ready advice on picture selection and the manuscript.

A classic BCT terminus. A couple of immaculate buses awaiting departure time, the Bundy time-recording clock standing sentry to ensure they did not leave early. Alongside is the neat shelter painted an unobtrusive green, relieved with cream, carrying a typical lollipop shaped stop plate. It's a red plate, indicating a compulsory stop as one would expect at a terminus. Most ordinary stops were blue request plates but red plates were placed at important locations and on downward gradients of steep hills to force drivers, at the very least, to slow down until conductors gave two rings on the bell for 'go'. Each driver had a key for the Bundy clock. Every key had a different number, thus identifying the driver. When he inserted and turned the key, it recorded the unique number and the time on a paper tape inside for an inspector to check. Passengers thought drivers loved the clocks so much that each one was happy to wind them up at every opportunity; the truth was rather different! This is 1953 Metro-Cammell-bodied Guy Arab IV 2986 at the Gospel Oak in 1969 — the bus has two spotlamps in anticipation of new regulations which, in the event, did not involve older buses. *Malcolm Keeley*

5

1. BIRMINGHAM FORMS TRANSPORT DEPARTMENT

At the beginning of the 20th century, there was a network of tramways in and around Birmingham, whose boundary was much smaller then. Whilst the tramcars were owned by the British Electric Traction Co Ltd, which ran tramways all over the UK, many of the local tramways on which they ran were leased from local authorities. When these leases expired, some local authorities such as Birmingham decided to run their own tramcars over the lines, electrifying them if they had not already been converted.

The first Birmingham Corporation Tramways operation began on 4 January 1904, following the expiry of the BET's Aston lease. Twenty new electric bogie cars began work between Steelhouse Lane, in the city centre, and the city boundary at Aston Brook Street, operating out of a depot in Miller Street. The most astonishing date, however, must have been 1 January 1907 when new Corporation-worked electric tram routes were introduced in many parts of the city. Some routes were completely new, others replaced BET City of Birmingham Tramway operations, mainly previously employing steam-hauled trams.

No buses were bought between 1916 and 1922, and then AEC dominated bus orders for the next decade. Birmingham introduced top-covered double-deckers in 1924, ahead of any other operator at this time. The leading vehicle here, No 123, was one of Birmingham's first production batch of 30 AEC 504 models, and is seen being washed at Acocks Green garage, opened in June 1928 when this picture was probably taken. Behind is No 283, a 1927 ADC 507 model, showing some of the recent developments, notably pneumatic tyres and enclosed cab. ADC was a short-lived partnership of AEC and Daimler. Short Bros bodied most of these vehicles but 283 belonged to a batch of 10 with Vickers bodies. *Birmingham City Transport*

Short Bros was a pioneer of metal-framed bus bodies, supplying its first to Birmingham in 1927 on this ADC 507, No 285, seen descending the hill on College Road, Wake Green. It had flush one-piece lower side panels without a rocker panel and, strangely by this time, an open-cab. A production batch of Short metal-framed bodies was supplied over the winter of 1928/9 on ADC 507s 296-337. These accorded more closely in external appearance to Birmingham's other 507s with enclosed cabs and split side panels. Bus services were numbered 1 upwards as if the tram network did not exist but avoided duplicating numbers along the same roads. *Courtesy H. Stone/ The Transport Museum, Wythall*

Motorbus operation had begun on 19 July 1913, from Selly Oak to Rednal, when BCT only had powers to operate them as extensions to tramway services. Wider powers were gained and more substantial bus operations, along the Hagley Road and to Harborne, Moseley and Browne's Green (Handsworth Wood Rd/Friary Rd), came following an agreement in 1914 with the bus company Midland Red (proper name Birmingham & Midland Motor Omnibus Company, often known as BMMO), created by the British Electric Traction Co Ltd in 1904. This agreement ensured Midland Red and the local authority did not compete wastefully with each other. It served us Brummies well, as the Corporation buses provided the local services whilst Midland Red in due course effectively offered a limited stop alternative down most of the major arteries on their way to destinations beyond the city boundary. As part of the deal, Birmingham Corporation acquired 30 Tilling-Stevens double-deckers from the company and a garage in Tennant Street.

Motorbuses began to arrive in quantity in 1922, the same year also saw an experimental trolleybus installation introduced to the Nechells service. On 24 July 1924, the General Manager, Mr Alfred Baker, was pleased to place into service what he claimed to be the first 'modern' top-covered double-decker, all previous ones being open. Over 200 similar vehicles on AEC/ADC 504 and 507 chassis were purchased up until 1929, including some with lowheight bodies for the Inner Circle service, and bus garages across the city were opened to accommodate them.

Like many cities, Birmingham was considering replacement of its tramways by buses. The first substantial experiment was at the beginning of 1934 when Leyland trolleybuses took over on the Coventry Road. Although more trolleybuses were purchased for the Nechells and Coventry Road services, it was concluded that trolleybuses were as route-bound as the tramways and motorbuses were the way forward. The tramway replacement programme proper began at the beginning of 1937 with the Stratford Road and Warwick Road services. The Stratford Road tramway was already duplicated over much of its length by bus routes serving new housing estates.

The deal with Midland Red involved the transfer of 30 Tilling-Stevens TTA1 and TTA2 double-deck buses to the Corporation in October 1914. The TTA1 models had smaller 30hp engines which lacked zest. Five were fitted in 1916 with new Brush 25-seat bodies, No 11 being shown here; the original double-deck bodies passing to new, more powerful, Tilling-Stevens TS3 chassis. In 1919, the single-deck bodies were transferred to the TS3 chassis, with the result that the 'Box Tillies', as they were known, were quite well spoken of with better power to weight ratio than the double-deckers. *MRK Collection*

The Corporation purchased a total of 30 Guy Conquest normal-control single-deckers in 1929/30 with Guy's own 26-seat bodies. They were returned to Guy in the winter of 1931/2 for rebuilding as 32-seat forward-control buses. Unrebuilt No 57 is seen alongside modernised No 54 (OF 3963) which seems to be missing its front registration plate. BCT liked to keep its single-deckers numbered below 90 in the interwar years. *MRK Collection*

2. THE FLEET IN 1937

The undertaking had changed its name in 1927 to Birmingham Corporation Tramway & Omnibus Dept. By 1937, its future was clearly wedded to buses so the tramway reference was dropped in favour of Birmingham City Transport from 9 November. Let us review the fleet at that time.

Tramcars

There are those who say all Birmingham buses looked the same. This is nonsense, of course, but the comment is an unintended tribute to the visual strength of the proud livery they carried which submerged the differences between the classes. The same comment is also made about Birmingham's trams, one wonders with a bit more justification until one reads the masterly work by P. W. Lawson, detailing the constant improvements applied to them. Mr Lawson described Birmingham's policy as standardisation without stagnation. True for buses and trams — Birmingham was not sidetracked by fashion, leading to batches of disaster vehicles with short lives; it energetically tested new ideas and adopted the best.

Birmingham's trams ran on a narrow gauge of 3ft 6in, due to the unhelpful width of many streets in which they operated. The original trams, Nos 1-20, were double-deck bogie cars built in 1904 with open-cabs (known as vestibules) and open-tops. Top-covers were soon fitted but leaving the ends of the upper-deck (the balconies) open. The vestibules were enclosed in the 1920s to give the driver some weather protection. All these trams were still in service in 1937 but largely restricted to the Perry Barr 6 route on account of their height.

Doubts about the ability of bogie cars to handle Birmingham's gradients meant that the next cars were four-wheelers. Moreover they were of shorter length, identifiable by only three side windows; 21-70 were new in 1905 and further examples, 221-300, followed in 1906 and 1908. They were intended for routes with difficult turns or height restrictions. The latter ceased to be a problem after

the top-covered but lower 301 class could take over routes with height problems. It was then possible to equip 21-70 and 221-300 with top-covers, retaining open balconies, all but one being done between 1911 and 1925. Most, but not all, received enclosed vestibules in the 1920s. These smaller cars were prime candidates for withdrawal under the earlier conversions and only 17 remained in passenger use by the end of 1937. These were retained for the tortuous Lodge Road 32 route, worked out of Rosebery Street depot.

The Board of Trade relaxed its view on top-covers on 3ft 6in gauge tramcars in sufficient time for 71-220, built in 1906, to be delivered with them. These four-wheelers were longer with four side windows and used on routes without height restrictions. The lower-saloon platforms were enclosed with vestibules in the 1920s and all but one were still in use at the end of 1937.

Tramcars 301-400 and 401-50 were received under three contracts between 1911 and 1913, again four-wheelers and, as mentioned above, a reduced height to give them wide

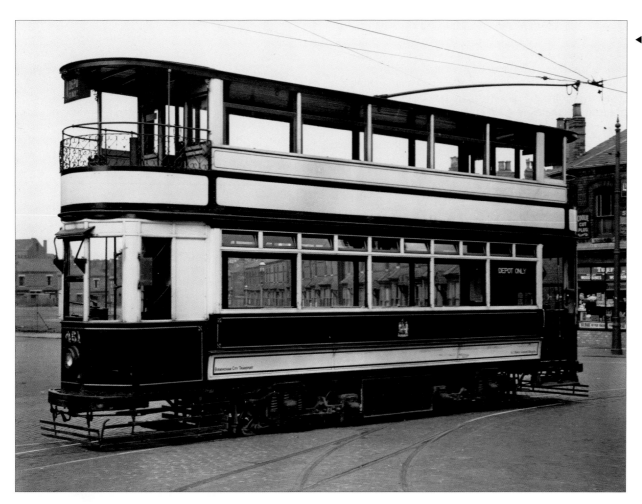

availability around the system despite top covers. They were the first to be delivered with enclosed vestibules so now only the balconies remained fully open to the elements. Nos 342 and 347 received experimental enclosed balconies in 1921 but the rest remained open.

Nos 451-511 were tramcars taken over from the BET-owned City of Birmingham Tramways upon expiry or purchase of the leases of certain tram lines serving districts added to Birmingham in 1911. Many were in poor condition but subsequently some were upgraded to BCT standards with open balcony top-covers and platform vestibules, and were not withdrawn until 1937-9. The others were converted to permanent way vehicles or scrapped fairly early on.

▶ Nos 451-2, however, became celebrity vehicles on the system. They were bogie cars new in 1903 and, at around 34ft in length and with five windows per side, were the longest trams BCT operated. BCT selected them to be amongst several cars experimentally (and unsuccessfully) converted to single-deckers with trailers, at this time receiving vestibules. Nos 451-2 were rebuilt as splendid top-covered double-deckers with open balconies in the 1920s and as such were to have long lives alongside the original bogie cars on the Perry Barr 6 route.

Subsequent trams belonged to a new generation. Design improvements meant previous doubts about bogie cars climbing steep gradients were removed. New bogie cars would be longer and could seat 62, compared to 54 of the 401 class four-wheeler. Nos 512-86 were delivered in 1913/14 with open balconies. Up until and including this contract, all tramcars purchased new had UEC bodies and Dick, Kerr equipment. World War 1 had interrupted the development of the system and, when deliveries resumed, the body and equipment suppliers would vary with successive contracts. The first postwar deliveries were 587-636, entering service in 1920/1 with open balconies. The next contract, 637-61 of 1923, were the first to be built with enclosed balconies and, over the next few years, 512-636 would be similarly improved. More orders took the fleet numbers up to 731 by January 1926. Further tramcars, 732-841, were built between 1926 and 1929 but differed in specifying air brakes, and 762 onwards incorporated much shorter windows upstairs. Nos 762-811 were fitted with bow collectors instead of trolley poles and were particularly associated with Washwood Heath depot.

Two experimental lightweight bogie cars were built in 1929/30 and numbered 842/3. Bodied by Short and Brush respectively, the builders produced quite different designs but both were striking in appearance. These experiments indicated intentions for a new generation of Birmingham tramcars but it was not to be and they were the end of the line. Nos 842/3 settled in alongside 812-41 at Cotteridge and remained unique.

Representing the general appearance of around 300 of Birmingham's later tramcars, 792 was one of 50 built by Brush on EMB Burnley bogies in 1928. This particular series was associated for 22 years with Washwood Heath depot where they had bow collectors instead of trolley poles. It is seen in May 1929 at the outer terminus of tram service 10, at the junction of Washwood Heath Road and Bromford Lane (the Outer Circle).
Birmingham City Transport

The last new tramcars were two experimental lightweights that entered service in 1929/30. No 842 was the first and had a Short Bros 63-seat body on lightweight English Electric Burnley bogies and two Dick, Kerr 40hp motors, offering a considerable reduction in current consumption compared to the 63hp motors latterly specified. The very prominent louvred vents over the lower-deck windows were fitted in 1930 after complaints from passengers about poor ventilation. Maley & Taunton bogies were fitted from accident-damaged tram 821 upon motor failure in 1950. This view dates from the 1930s.
J. E. Cull

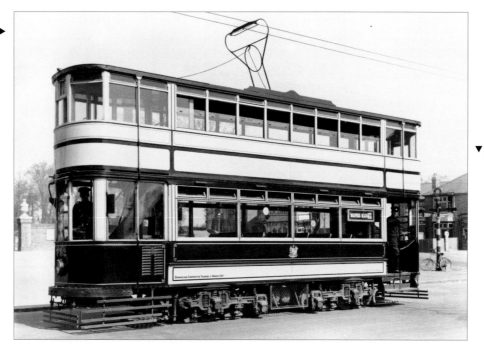

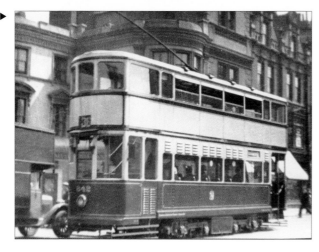

Five of these AEC Mercury tower wagons, delivered in 1934, assisted the needs of the tram and trolleybus overhead department. Maintenance close to home is being carried out at Selly Oak depot with trams 558 and 833 forming the background. Two of these tower wagons passed to Walsall Corporation for its trolleybus system after Birmingham's last trams were withdrawn in 1953.
G. H. Stone

The early trolleybuses built between 1922 and 1926 were replaced by new Leylands and AECs in 1932. There were 11 Leylands, delivered in February. They carried the numbers 1-3/5-7/9-11/3/5, avoiding the numbers of earlier trolleybuses retained in service until the AECs arrived. The five AECs followed in late summer 1932 as 12-16, with Leylands 13 and 15 being renumbered 4 and 8. It is thus certain that this picture of Leyland 15 was taken in 1932. The chassis were of the TBD1 type and looked extraordinarily like motorbuses, even having dummy radiators. The 48-seat bodies were by Short Bros. *R. T. Wilson*

Metro-Cammell-bodied Leyland TTBD2 59 is waiting at the original outer terminus of the Coventry Road trolleybus route at the Swan, Yardley in September 1934. *MRK Collection*

No 71, one of the 1937 delivery of Metro-Cammell-bodied Leyland TB5 trolleybuses, rolls past the entrance to Arthur Street (later renamed Coventry Road) depot, revealing the complex overhead. The khaki roof reveals this to be a post-World War 2 scene. *G. H. Stone*

Trolleybuses

The original generation of trolleybuses built from 1922 for the Nechells service had been replaced by new trolleybuses in 1932. Nos 1-11 were two-axle Leyland TBD1 models which were exceptionally interesting in that the bodies, by Short Bros, were half-cab and looked like motorbuses. The Leylands struggled to meet axle weight restrictions so the next batch, Brush-bodied AEC 663Ts 12-16, had three axles.

The Coventry Road tram conversion in January 1934 brought 50 new three-axle Leyland TTBD2 trolleybuses with Metro-Cammell bodies, numbered 17-66. The Coventry Road route was extended in 1936 from Yardley to the junction with Arden Oak Road, Sheldon, and additional trolleybuses were built the following year. Nos 67-78 were again Leylands with Metro-Cammell bodies but were TB5 models, reverting to two axles following relaxation of weight limits.

Motorbuses

The performance of the AEC/ADC 504 and 507 buses may have shown the superiority of the bus over the tram in handling the new estates being built between or beyond the tram routes but bus design was moving on rapidly and all were withdrawn by the end of 1937.

Leyland had introduced a new range of buses in 1927 and AEC reacted by headhunting Leyland's Chief Designer, Mr G. J. Rackham, to develop vehicles that would put it at the forefront of design and innovation. His first new design was the AEC Regent that took the Leyland Titan TD1 concept further with a more compact and tidier front end. A demonstration visit by the AEC Regent prototype impressed Birmingham and the chassis became the standard double-decker between 1929 and the beginning of 1932, with fleet numbers spread between 338 and 503. All except No 408 were delivered with petrol engines and crash gearboxes. Birmingham's Regents carried full-height bodies with enclosed staircases by various bodybuilders to a very distinctive and attractive piano-fronted design specified by the corporation. There was also a splendid near-relative, based on the three-axle AEC Renown chassis,

numbered 92 (fleet Nos 91-100 were used for prototypes and demonstrators). The Renown was withdrawn in 1937 and converted to a rather grand recovery vehicle.

The Department had shown interest in metal-framed bodies and this continued into the Regent era with two 1930 prototypes. No 96 began as a demonstrator bodied by Short, its high standard of internal finish earning it the nickname of the 'Showboat'. It was quickly purchased by Birmingham and numbered 368. The other, numbered 209, re-using the fleet number of a prematurely withdrawn Karrier, was of greater long-term significance by carrying a prototype Metro-Cammell metal-framed body. The body manufacturer was well-known as a railway carriage builder but felt it should diversify its business. Bringing railway

▲ The last AEC/ADC 504s and 507s were withdrawn in 1937 but around two dozen lived on as departmental vehicles. Former AEC 504 bus 189, new in 1926, was rebuilt as a lorry in 1935. *Birmingham City Transport*

13

The first 30 AEC Regents, 338-67, were delivered at the end of 1929. The modern-looking chassis design with powerful six-cylinder petrol engine was a major advance while the bodies moved ahead in several respects, notably the enclosed staircases. Birmingham felt staircase design could be improved further and No 344 had an experimental straight staircase that was considered to be much safer, with tumbling passengers much less likely to be deposited in the road. It also gave a generous platform area. The straight staircase was perfected in time for the next contract of Regents for 1930 and would be a feature of all double-deckers bodied to Birmingham's specification until the rear-engine era. The 1930 contract comprised 75 vehicles with the body order split between English Electric (369-408) and Vulcan (409-43). The bodies seated 48 with the exception of No 408 which until 1937 had an experimental AEC diesel engine and, in consequence, one seat less in the upper-saloon to meet stringent weight regulations. An interesting move in 1932, furthering the experiment with 'heavy oil' (diesel) buses, was fitting the body of 442 to a new Crossley Condor chassis registered OJ 5442. No 442 ran in its new form until 1937.

No 387 poses with its crew at the then terminus alongside Trittiford Park where Highfield Road meets Priory Road. This is an example of a picture taken by a professional photographer who evidently made a living illustrating people at work and offering copies to the staff. Several bus pictures have turned up, this one being given to the astonished author 40 years ago by a neighbour, Mr Flanagan, who was the conductor here. Who knows what still may be hidden in people's attics? *MRK Collection*

experience, it developed the most successful and widely copied steel bus structure, based on a 'top hat'-shaped pillar with a timber insert that made panel replacement easy. Metro-Cammell demonstrated the strength of its new design by shunting a railway truck into 209 to show the limited extent of damage and deflection!

The last petrol-engined Regents, 484-503, had similar Metro-Cammell bodies and metal frames became standard for the Corporation's new buses. Surprisingly, the very successful AEC era was drawing to an end in Birmingham. Alongside the Metro-Cammell Regents came 10 single-deck bodies from the same manufacturer but on Morris Dictator chassis. Worldwide trade depression encouraged support for local industry and Morris-Commercial buses were built in Birmingham. The ten Dictators, 81-90, were followed in 1933-4 by four more Dictators, 47-50 (later 77-80), and no less than 50 Morris Imperial double-deckers. All these had Morris's own petrol engines, driving through a crash gearbox. The design was revolutionary in that, after removing the radiator, the engine could be disconnected and wheeled out, an idea successfully revived on London Transport's Routemaster. Morris Imperials 504-6 had one-off bodies by Brush, English Electric and Gloucester RCW respectively; the remaining 47, numbered 507-53, had Metro-Cammell bodies.

The Morris buses were not well-regarded but the next 10 vehicles, 554-63, delivered in 1933-4, were Daimler CP6 models that broke new ground by incorporating Daimler's preselective gearboxes. This wonderful gearbox design had featured on a Daimler CH6 demonstrator tested from 1931 onwards, numbered 100 (VC 7519) whilst with BCT. It released drivers from the exactitude of the crash gearbox and would not stall. Creeping along congested city streets ceased to be agony for the left leg. Less impressive, however, were Daimler's own petrol engines. Bodies on 554-63 were by another famous local railway carriage builder, Birmingham Railway Carriage & Wagon (BRCW).

Many demonstrators were received from manufacturers anxious to attract the custom of this important operator. Latterly, like most major operators in the early 1930s, the corporation had become seriously interested in the diesel engines then being developed. Regent 408 had an experimental AEC diesel unit, described as reeking abominably in hot weather but the fastest bus in the city! It would be withdrawn in 1938, among the first Regents to go. Another Regent, 442, was re-chassised in 1932 with a diesel-powered Crossley Condor, lasting until the end of 1937. One of the earlier demonstrators was a Guy Invincible, 97 (UK 8047), which began an extended hire to Birmingham in December 1929. This Hall Lewis 48-seat bodied bus then had a Guy six-cylinder petrol engine. Guy fitted it with a Gardner 6LW diesel in 1932, no doubt as a trial for the new Arab model which was to be the first bus chassis in this country offered without a petrol engine alternative. UK 8047's hire ended in December 1933, the same month its 6LW was removed for fitting into a new Arab chassis frame. This chassis became a further one-off vehicle for Birmingham, numbered 208 (OC 8208), bodied by Metro-Cammell and entering service in May 1934. It reused the fleet number of a recently withdrawn earlier Guy, an experimental three-axle BKX.

The Gardner engine, in both 6LW and the smaller 5LW forms, became an option in Daimler's chassis with preselective gearbox. A visit by demonstration Daimler COG5 KV 1396 late in 1933 emphasised, even before Guy 208 entered service, that the 5LW-engined Daimler chassis would suit Birmingham Corporation down to the ground. Around 800 would be purchased in the years up to the outbreak of World War 2. Nos 564-963, 969-1033, 1039-139 were delivered between 1934 and 1937; 1139 being exhibited at the 1937 Commercial Motor Show. Bodies were mainly by Metro-Cammell and BRCW but there were small, single batches in 1935 by Northern Counties (674-88) and Short (689-93). Other COG5s were 45 single-deckers (Nos 32-76 with Metro-Cammell or Strachans bodies) built in 1935/6, and a front-entrance double-decker bodied by Metro-Cammell (numbered 94), the door position reflecting the then current preference of Midland Red but looking nothing like one of its buses, even though the bodybuilder was the same!

Daimler did not have a complete monopoly on orders, however. Leyland's 'gearless' Lysholm-Smith torque-

converter transmission interested the Corporation following a lengthy visit of 15 months in 1933/4 by Leyland TD2c demonstrator TF 7310 (numbered 94 by BCT). This was followed up by fitting the torque-converters to eight AEC Regents, 361-7 and 502, coupled to either Leyland or AEC diesel engines. Five complete Leyland TD4c buses, 964-8, were placed into service in May 1937, bodied by Leyland to its new standard design evolved by ex-Metro-Cammell man Colin Bailey, but modified to Birmingham specification. Around the time AEC lost its grip on Birmingham's orders, it began offering preselective transmission but had no luck with Birmingham until five were ordered for evaluation in 1937. Nos 1034-8 had AEC 7.7-litre engines (actually 7.585-litres but the marketing men liked the sound of seven-seven) and Metro-Cammell bodies.

▲ Rear view of 1930 AEC Regent 374, clearly showing its straight staircase. The enclosing of the staircases meant that passengers had limited escape from the upper-saloon in the event of the platform being crushed in an accident or overturning onto the nearside. The 1931 Regents would be the corporation's first buses to meet the new legal requirement of a fully opening upper-deck emergency window, located in the rear dome.
MRK Collection

Faced with devastating international economic and trade recession, train carriage and wagon manufacturer Metropolitan-Cammell added bus bodies to its portfolio in 1930. Prototype bodies with a new design of metal frame were produced that year, Birmingham taking one on AEC Regent chassis as bus 209. Birmingham's 1931 Regents comprised 60 vehicles, 444-83 having timber framed bodies, this time by Short, while 484-503 had all-metal bodies by Metro-Cammell, identifiable by their unradiused windows. The bodies were so successful that Metro-Cammell became a market leader. *Metro-Cammell*

Forty-seven of the 50 Morris Imperials, delivered in 1933/4, had Metro-Cammell bodies, including 514 seen at the Yew Tree, Yardley, on a very warm day – just look at those refreshing open ventilators! The Imperials had very tidy front profiles and arguably looked more modern than many of the buses that followed. *MRK Collection*

16

One of the most radical demonstrators received was the side-engined AEC Q. AHX 63 was the prototype double-deck AEC Q, built in 1932 and seated 31 upstairs and 29 down. Historians are still debating the bodybuilder, with Metro-Cammell and Park Royal being speculated. AEC's record card shows it as LGOC (London General), a BCT file note records the upholstery as LGOC and it shares many styling features with London United trolleybus 61, also bodied by LGOC. Built with a petrol engine, it worked in Birmingham for a year beginning January 1933, carrying the number 93 in the experimental series. It returned to the manufacturer, reappearing in Birmingham with an AEC diesel engine during January 1935, and was purchased by the Corporation in October. Its revolutionary design was too early for the industry as a whole but one detail feature of its body evidently impressed Birmingham! The softly curved belt rails below the windows and at upper-deck floor level was adopted from Daimler COG5 594 and retained until the end of standard Birmingham half-cab bus production in 1954. No 93 was sold via a dealer to Herefordshire operator Yeomans in 1940. *AEC*

The standard bus between 1934 and 1939 was the Daimler COG5 with frugal Gardner 5LW diesel engine, mostly with Metro-Cammell bodies. A large minority, however, were bodied by Birmingham Railway Carriage & Wagon (BRCW). Prewar in-service views of the earliest COG5s, 564-93, are rare. The first 15 were BRCW-bodied; this is 567 (AOB 567) in Bull Street on 29 August 1934, like all 30 of the first batch working from Harborne garage. *R. T. Wilson*

The next 100 COG5s completed the transformation to the style most associated with BCT half-cabs, with the introduction of raised belt rails edged in herzim mouldings. The mouldings included a straw coloured plastic insert. This arrangement replaced the black lining previously applied to the cream and the gold on the dark blue, apart from the bus bonnet. The lining continued to be reapplied to repainted earlier buses into World War 2. No less than four bodybuilders benefited from this contract, Metro-Cammell (594-633), BRCW (634-73), Northern Counties (674-88) and Short (689-93). All were delivered over the winter of 1934-5, except the Northern Counties examples which did not arrive until the spring. Nos 594-628 were allocated to Selly Oak but 629-93 joined the first series at Harborne. No 605 waits in Navigation Street in July 1935. *R. T. Wilson*

How kind of the Harborne garage staff to choose one of the rare Short-bodied COG5s, 689-93, to pose alongside! There is a slight radius to the window corners, unlike the bodies from other coachbuilders. Birmingham had an excellent relationship with Daimler; not only was the Coventry manufacturer relatively local but it was a two-way conversation between the two organisations, both determined to improve the breed. Chief Engineer Mr T. Rowland and his deputy and successor, Mr H. Parker, patented several devices including, in the mid-1930s, automatic lubrication and automatic brake adjusters. Clayton Dewandre had sole marketing rights for these, sold under the initials RP of the two engineers. *The Transport Museum, Wythall archive*

Visitors and outpatients to today's bustling Queen Elizabeth Hospital, in the southwest of the city, have the choice of bus and rail public transport, or the use of large car parks. This prewar view of COG5/Metro-Cammell 43 suggests a more placid scene – the destination blind shows the then name of the hospital. There were 45 Daimler COG5 single-deckers, numbered 32-76, bodied by Metro-Cammell or Strachans. They seated 34 and maintained the policy of numbering single-deckers below 90. *MRK Collection*

A number of operators were experimenting with forward-entrance double-deckers in the mid-1930s, most particularly Midland Red which standardised on the layout for the rest of the decade. No 94 with body by Metro-Cammell was demonstrated in 1936 to the corporation which purchased it. It ran until 31 October 1950, always from Acocks Green on the 1/1A service. For the first few years it would have had AEC Q No 93 for company. *MRK Collection*

Leyland had a good reputation for coachwork until its first metal-framed bodies in 1934-5 which were disastrous. Metro-Cammell designer Colin Bailey was headhunted by Leyland and he introduced an elegant body style that would prove extremely successful. Birmingham's 1937 trial batch of Leyland Titan TD4c buses, 964-8, with so-called 'gearless' torque-converter transmission, were fitted with Leyland's new design of body, modified to include some of Birmingham's preferences, such as straight staircases, swivelling cab windows and lower-saloon front-bulkhead ventilators. *Leyland*

The five 1937 AEC Regents with preselector gearboxes, 1034-8, could have led to big contracts as alternative supplier to BCT but Leyland won. The bodies were by Metro-Cammell, similar to the COG5s but with a sloping lower edge to the windscreen. This is a 1949 view of 1038, in Old Square, with Daimler CVG6 1915, then very new. Both were running from Liverpool Street garage. 1034-8 were to have a new engine design but it proved disappointing in a test chassis. 7-7 direct injection engines were fitted instead, including the test chassis which ran for a year with the body of 483 registered DOB 483.
Roy Marshall

19

3. TRAMWAYS INTO BLACK COUNTRY REPLACED

The only tram services normally entering the city after 1912 not owned by the Corporation were those of two BET companies, the South Staffs Tramways from Darlaston (extended to Bilston from 1923) via West Bromwich, and the Birmingham District Power & Traction, operating from Dudley via Smethwick.

As the BET tramway leases through West Bromwich began to expire in 1924, that corporation asked Birmingham Corporation to extend the Soho Road trams across the boundary through West Bromwich and replace the South Staffs trams to Dudley and Wednesbury — the section between that town and Bilston being transferred to Wolverhampton District Electric Tramways. When the question was raised subsequently about replacing the tramways with buses, West Bromwich decided to run its

own vehicles. West Bromwich, in fact, was rather keen on trolleybuses but motorbuses won the day and the Dudley and Wednesbury services became a joint Birmingham/West Bromwich operation when all the Soho Road tram services were replaced by motorbuses from 2 April 1939. The conductors' waybills had to be reopened at the boundary and the passengers paid again until as late as 1967 when a more sensible arrangement was introduced, splitting the revenue by formula.

In 1928, by agreement with Birmingham District, Birmingham Corporation trams took over the route to Dudley via Smethwick, for the time being having a monopoly of the Dudley Road services. By 1 January 1939, the BET leases in Dudley had expired and the other local authorities outside Birmingham compulsorily purchased

No 226, one of the 85 Metro-Cammell-bodied Leyland TD6c Titans purchased to replace the Soho Road trams, loads at the shelters in Colmore Row, outside the main entrance to Snow Hill railway station, soon after the conversion. Describing the 69 as a Soho Road service is a bit of a misnomer as it branched into Great Hampton Row before the main road became Soho Road. Delivery of these buses began in December 1938 and most were bedded in at Acocks Green garage, moving to Hockley upon the conversion.
The Omnibus Society

Bodies for FOF-registered Daimler COG5 buses 1140-1236 under construction at Metro-Cammell in 1939.
The Transport Museum, Wythall archive

the remainder so that the trams could be replaced. However they arranged for the replacement services to be operated by buses of BET subsidiary Midland Red. The Dudley Road out of Birmingham thus became jointly operated; basically BCT ran the B80-B83 to Grove Lane, Bearwood and Soho, and Midland Red the B84-B89 to Smethwick, Oldbury and Dudley, a reflection of the pre-1928 arrangements, although there were exceptions to balance the mileage between the corporation and Midland Red. The B-prefix was part of Midland Red's route numbering system, indicating a Birmingham local service. This was a controversial conversion as the buses took over on 1 October 1939, after the outbreak of World War 2 the previous month, meaning electric vehicles using home-produced energy were replaced by buses dependent on imported fuel. Replacement of the Ladywood and Lodge Road trams, intended at the same time, and the Stechford routes proposed for 1940 were deferred, however. The 1939 conversions saw the retirement of the 71-220 class of tramcars, built in 1906.

The 1938 bus deliveries reused fleet numbers of earlier buses already sold. Daimler COG5s were 102-200 (it is thought that 1139 was to have been numbered 101), whilst 1140-1269 comprised the 1939 COG5 order. Bodies were again mostly Metro-Cammell and BRCW but there were one-off bodies by English Electric, Park Royal and Brush on 1237-9. 1937's alternative suppliers were being tested for the big orders to replace the tramway routes into the Black Country. Leyland won the contracts, the first being for 85 TD6c torque-converter-fitted chassis and Metro-Cammell bodies, seating only 52 to comply with weight limits. Guy 208 and Regent 209 were still in service so these reused vacant numbers 211-95. Delivery began in December 1938 and most were settled in at Acocks Green garage prior to the whole lot replacing the Soho Road tramways from Hockley garage in April 1939. A second batch of TD6c buses, 1270-1319, replaced the Dudley Road trams. This time Leyland 52-seat bodies were fitted; like 964-8 they had Birmingham modifications. However the standard Leyland body had moved on, with radiused windows and a rounded rear dome — these were very handsome buses.

◄ Had bus construction continued uninterrupted, it is likely that COG5s from 1940 onwards would have had radiused windows. Metro-Cammell bodied 1236 had some windows so treated, and the experimental bodies on 1238 by Park Royal and 1239 by Brush were largely radiused, as were all the Leyland-bodied TD6c buses. This is 1238 which, like 1237, did not enter service until 1 March 1940. This explains the white guardrail for the wartime blackout but the roof is still cream, a camouflage colour to make vehicles less obvious in air raids was soon adopted. *MRK Collection*

◄ More Leyland TD6c buses were received for the Dudley Road conversion. This time Leyland bodies were favoured, the incorporation of BCT features into the manufacturer's standard bodyshell producing some very attractive vehicles. This is a postwar view of 1309 on football duties, at the head of a line of COG5 and TD6c buses. *D. Morris/ courtesy T. W. Moore*

4. WORLD WAR 2

No less than 1,170 employees joined the armed forces upon the declaration of war with a consequent effect on performance. Services were reduced to conserve fuel, tyres etc and many single-deckers were converted to ambulances. Bus roofs were soon painted khaki to reduce their visibility to enemy aircraft. The motorbus fleet was comparatively modern; AEC Regent buses dating back as far as 1929 were still in stock but their numbers were diminishing and dwarfed by the big contracts for tramway replacement buses delivered in the three years before the war. Sadly the 1933/4 Morris buses had proved unreliable and many were delicensed as war broke out, but some returned to service as other buses had to be taken off the road.

BCT had ordered another 12 Metro-Cammell-bodied Leyland two-axle trolleybuses to permit replacement of the 1932 Leylands. These TB7 models were delivered early in 1940 and numbered 79-90 (FOK 79-90). It is now known that most of the 1932 Leylands were stored from this time and some of the 67-78 batch moved to the Nechells 7 service. However, the Nechells trolleybuses were suddenly replaced by motorbuses after 30 September 1940. Trolleybuses returning to Washwood Heath depot via the tram route had to trail a metal skate along the tram rail for the electrical return. This caused unacceptable flashing under the blackout regulations. It was intended to be only a temporary suspension and conductors continued to be

No 16, one of the five AEC 663T trolleybuses with Brush 58-seat bodies built in 1932, at the Nechells terminus in Cuckoo Road, on 24 February 1940. Note the masked headlights. These had three axles following the axle weight problems with the preceding Leylands.
L. W. Perkins/courtesy F. A. Wycherley

24

supplied by Washwood Heath until March 1946 but trolleybuses never returned to Nechells. The replacing bus route, worked by Liverpool Street garage, was numbered 43 as there was already a 7 bus route to Portland Road. All trolleybuses between 1-16 still in service were thus placed into store while, by the end of 1940, all of 17-90 were engaged on the Coventry Road. The latter operation was extended from 29 October 1941 with an additional branch from the Wheatsheaf to the Rover works on Lode Lane in Solihull. This was an exceptional circumstance, being into Solihull and thus Midland Red territory but permitted to save imported fuel.

Considerable loss of life and damage was incurred in the city during air raids, affecting its residents, including BCT's employees. Tram routes often had to be suspended, not only because of actual damage but also due to unexploded bombs in the vicinity or debris and fire hoses across the tracks. The fleet suffered too, notably in air raids which hit Highgate Road and Hockley bus garages and Witton tram depot in 1940, and Miller Street and Washwood Heath tram depots in the most serious raid on the city in April 1941. The tram losses included 14 of the original 20 tramcars of 1904. In contrast, at Hockley, six modern Leylands were completely destroyed in the raid that also rendered a considerable number of bus bodies beyond repair. The top decks of four of the Metro-Cammell-bodied Imperials were used to replace blitz-damaged top decks on two Daimler COG5 (912/27) and two Leyland-bodied Leyland TD6c vehicles (1281/3).

The Department took the opportunity in September 1941 to purchase 20 English Electric bodies intended for Manchester Corporation and built to its very distinctive design. The chassis for these had been destroyed in a raid on the Daimler factory in Coventry. By June 1942 12 had been fitted to Leyland TD6c chassis (214/5/7/25/31/5/7/41/9/59/73/93) and four more to Daimler COG5s to replace written off bodies (two as direct replacements on 1018 and 1133, and two on 814 and 918 whose original bodies were repaired and fitted to 901 and 1010, the bodies of which had been lost). Bodies took longer to overhaul than chassis, particularly with the

backlog of body maintenance during the war. The remaining four were fitted in 1942/3 to Daimler COG5s 727/65, 820/42 to create a float of bodies. Buses thus entered the works and their bodies were lifted off. Overhauled chassis would receive the first overhauled body available, enabling chassis to be returned to service more quickly. Many Daimler COG5 chassis had at least one body swap around this period.

Four Metro-Cammell-bodied Daimler COG6 buses intended for Johannesburg, South Africa, were received by BCT and entered service as Nos 1320-3 over the winter of 1941/2. These had not been shipped due to the activity of German submarines. The need for new buses across the country was becoming critical so manufacturers were allowed to complete vehicles already partly constructed. BCT thus received eight Leyland TD7 buses with crash gearboxes in 1942. 1324-6/9-31 had Leyland bodies to the manufacturer's peacetime standard but 1327/8 were the department's first taste of wartime 'austerity' bodies, specified by the Ministry of Supply. 1327 was bodied by Park Royal and 1328 by Northern Coach Builders.

This was then followed by the limited production of new buses, all with austerity bodies and allocated to operators by the Ministry of War Transport. Only Guy and Daimler were involved initially, later Bristol was added. Operators

▲ The 1937 Leyland TB5 trolleybuses were moving onto the Nechells route when the sudden conversion to motorbuses occurred. No 78 looks extremely smart in this view. *G. Kelland collection*

Crouching to minimise glare from the sun, the photographer captures some nice cars in Albert Street as well as Leyland TB7 trolleybus No 84, one of the 12 delivered in 1940. *R. T. Wilson*

▲ had little influence over what they received and there was minimal effort at standardising deliveries. Only 149 further buses, numbered 1332-1480, were received by BCT between 1942 and the beginning of 1946, some months after the war ended: 84 were Guy Arabs with Gardner 5LW engines, the latter very familiar to BCT. Three Daimler CWG5s, which were a wartime version of the COG5, were similarly Gardner-powered. Daimler was then obliged to switch over to AEC 7.7 engines so 55 wartime Daimlers were CWA6 models. Daimler's own CD6 diesel engine was developed by the end of the war and these units were fitted to seven CWD6 buses. All the Daimlers had preselective gearboxes but the Guys had formidable crash boxes. The Guys and Daimlers were bodied by a wide selection of builders. Many had wooden slatted seats and some were delivered in grey primer; a number of existing buses were similarly painted as camouflage. Manufacturers were allowed to build prototypes for postwar production and two Guys, 1378 and 1384, beneath the surface of austerity had experimental metal-framed Weymann bodies with radiused windows.

With the limited delivery of new buses, the poor durability of the timber frame bodies on the surviving 1929-31 AEC Regents became a serious problem. Fifty thus received new Brush 'austerity' bodies in 1943/4; BCT considered delivery was slow. Brush had quoted for complete bodies with cost reductions for items salvaged from the old ones such as seats, staircases, windscreens, destination gear, light fittings, bells and bell pushes. A major dispute broke out over the cost. The dismantling and salvaging of the old bodies used up scarce labour, disrupted Brush's production line and delayed delivery. The old bodies were by four different manufacturers, causing unexpected additional detailed design work to re-use the salvaged materials. Brush thus claimed that the salvaging had increased rather than reduced the body prices. Despite this, in February 1944, BCT confirmed with AEC that chassis spares would continue to be manufactured and, towards the end of the war, more bodies were separated from chassis. It seems likely that further rebodies would have occurred if the war had continued.

Manchester Corporation matchstriker from a rebodied Birmingham COG5! *Roy Hennefer*

◄ Wartime blitz devastation at Highgate Road garage. *Birmingham Post & Mail*

▼ No 225 was one of 12 blitz-damaged Leyland TD6c buses fitted with English Electric bodies purchased from Manchester Corporation. This view of it at Snow Hill station makes an interesting direct comparison with 226 on page 20. *The Transport Museum, Wythall*

Bus 842 was badly damaged by enemy action in 1940 and was one of eight Daimler COG5s fitted with 'Manchester' bodies. The body was transferred in 1949 to No 978. This fine view in High Street shows the latter awaiting departure time before turning right into New Street for a north side only journey on the cross-city Highfield Road (Hall Green) to Kingstanding service. The bus was probably working for Birchfield Road garage at the time.
◄◄ *Michael Rooum*

The lower saloons of four blitz-damaged buses were salvageable so the upper-decks were replaced by those from withdrawn Morris Imperials. The two mounted on Leyland lower decks did not fit at all well, their upright windscreens meaning the Morris upper decks were too short, as exemplified by 1283 here. This wartime view shows the practice of overnight parking buses around the suburbs to minimise similar destruction again should a garage be hit. *MRK Collection*

The driver's hand signal indicates that 'Johannesburg' Daimler COG6 1321 is about to pull across the carriageway in Victoria Square to be positioned correctly for Paradise Street in March 1948. The Metro-Cammell bodies were built with full-drop windows to cope with the South African heat but Tyburn Road Works in 1946 prevented them from opening beyond the half way position; 1322 at some point received half-drop ventilators. *John Edgington*

The exotic 1320-3 were 8ft wide, 6in wider than permitted in the UK under normal circumstances. They were not originally allowed in the city centre and thus were allocated to Yardley Wood for the inter-suburban 18 service between Haunch Lane and the further reaches of Northfield. Postwar width relaxation allowed them to be reallocated to service 9 and Harborne garage where this view of the rears of two rare buses was taken of 'Johannesburg' 1323 and Northern Counties-bodied COG5 687. *R. A. Mills*

Six of the eight Leyland Titan TD7s of 1942 had Leyland's own handsome bodywork to peacetime standards. All eight TD7s were allocated to Perry Barr garage where 1331 waits to be parked. The little window at the top of the cab door was a BCT addition to improve visibility, it was a plain panel when built by Leyland. 1324-6 had bodies originally intended for Lincoln Corporation while 1329-31 were initially expected to be bodied by Duple. *S. E. Letts*

The first Leyland TD7 into service was 1327 in January 1942. Originally allocated an East Lancs body, this was the only Birmingham TD7 bodied by Park Royal and introduced the joys of Ministry of Supply wartime austerity specification. It only ran until the end of 1948, just under seven years, during a period when photography by ordinary mortals was extremely difficult. This early postwar picture is thus exceptionally rare, showing it working the Outer Circle in Lordswood Road, about to turn right at the King's Head into Hagley Road. The sliding ventilators were fitted early in 1945.
N. S. Stone/courtesy G. H. Stone

Leyland TD7 1328 carried a relatively rare Northern Coachbuilders austerity body. It stands on the exit drive of Perry Barr garage with destination blind for the 29A Baldwins Lane (Hall Green) to Kingstanding service.
R. A. Mills

Under instruction from the Ministry of War Transport, 25 AEC Regents were converted in 1942/3 to run on gas produced by trailers burning anthracite to conserve supplies of imported fuel. They were operated by Perry Barr garage and used on service 33 to Kingstanding, including the ascent of Kingstanding Road hill. Performance was pretty dire and they were withdrawn or converted to normal as soon as possible. AEC Regent/Metro-Cammell 484 demonstrates the first installation. *Birmingham City Transport*

Austerity bodies with straight staircases were probably unique to Birmingham, thanks to the Brush rebuilds. No 469 is seen here; the new style of fleet number indicates this shot dates after early postwar repainting. *MRK Collection*

The 50 petrol-engined AEC Regents rebodied by Brush in 1943/4 were transformed in appearance. Clearly visible is the reused destination gear from the old bodies, hence the blind apertures were narrower than in the austerity bodies on new chassis. The recycled seats were upholstered, of course, unlike the slatted seats of new buses. The old English Electric, Vulcan and Short bodies had straight staircases and formed the majority of the Regents presented for rebodying. Brush produced bodies with these staircases first, although in some cases mounting them on the chassis of 1929 Regents whose old bodies, also built by Brush, had curved staircases. The two staircase styles were thus intermingled numerically but an external clue identifying a straight staircase was the short window at the rear offside, seen here on 477. *MRK Collection*

1944 Guy Arab II 1367 was one of many fitted with Weymann bodies and equipped with slatted wooden seats when new, receiving upholstered ones from withdrawn buses in 1946-8. It stands on the forecourt of Selly Oak garage in April 1949. *J. Cull/courtesy The Omnibus Society*

The body of this newly overhauled 1945 Daimler CWA6, 1389, was nearly scrapped after this 1947 accident but the original bodybuilder, Park Royal, was prevailed upon to repair it at an economic price. It belonged to a batch, 1385-92, with a sorry history. The Ministry of War Transport was not adept at standardising deliveries to operators but did invite them to state preferences. BCT favoured Weymann, Brush or Park Royal bodies, despite them only being available with timber frames, and did not appreciate it when eight Northern Counties-bodied Daimlers were allocated, to have been 1385-92. Northern Counties were building metal-frame bodies, which would prove robust, but BCT disapproved of the design and the buses were sent to other operators. Replacements were to be bodied by Brush as were a further 13 for 1944 delivery, 1413-25. Following on from the delivery delays and the dispute over prices for the AEC Regent rebodies, Brush managed to convince itself that the buses were for 1945, offering delivery to commence in June of that year. A frustrated BCT got the body contract for all 21 transferred to Park Royal which delivered them in the first half of 1945. As will be seen, their lives with BCT were not long. Brush did finally body four Daimlers, 1471-4. *Birmingham City Transport*

5. GETTING BACK TO NORMAL

By the beginning of 1946, all remaining petrol-engined Regents in passenger service carried Metro-Cammell bodies (and inroads had been made into these) or 1943/4 Brush bodies. Four more remained on the road with timber-framed bodies, however. These had been converted to dual-control training buses in 1938; the former 388, 339, 414 (by now carrying a replacement body ex-381, transferred in 1944) and 416 being numbered 55-8 in the service vehicle fleet. Of these, No 55 received the Metro-Cammell all-metal body from 498 in October 1947.

Some Morris Imperials were off the road at the outbreak of war and most of the remainder, together with the Daimler CP6s and Guy 208, were replaced by the limited deliveries of wartime buses. Only 521, 539 and 544 remained operational as 1946 opened.

Several complete COG5s had been judged beyond economic repair by the end of 1945, especially from the small 1935 batch bodied by Northern Counties. Also, one by one, the float of four bodies was used up, the last in 1948. On the positive side one additional body was the postwar prototype, built by Brush in 1946 and mounted on the chassis of 1235. The single-deck COG5 buses converted to ambulances or standee layout reverted to 34-seat standard in 1945/6 but five of the Strachans-bodied examples were withdrawn in 1946 and sold.

The last resumptions of services cut in wartime were reintroduced on 29 January 1946 and the last delivery of wartime design buses entered service the following month (Daimlers 1475-80). A new facility introduced on 15 April 1946 was all-night services with a minimum fare of 6d (2½p). Large destination boards were carried in front upper-saloon windows until details could be included on blinds. Several night services were extended in length in 1947 to take advantage of the mileage that could be covered within a round journey of an hour. Certain journeys on two routes were extended well beyond the city boundary; these being the NS80 to Grove Lane extended as the NS85 to Spon Lane, and the NS72 to Handsworth as

the NS73 to Carters Green by arrangement with West Bromwich Corporation.

Washwood Heath remained primarily a tram depot but, until 1940, had also operated the Nechells trolleybuses that were never reinstated after the wartime emergency. The replacing No 43 bus service was operated out of Liverpool Street garage. Rather than Washwood Heath take back the Nechells service, the depot received from 19 August 1946 an allocation of 22 buses (COG5s 126-36 and CWA6s 1385-92, 1413-5) to assist Liverpool Street on service 14 to Tile Cross.

The tram services worked from Rosebery Street depot were converted to motorbuses in 1947. Firstly, after 30 March, the Lodge Road tramway service 32 was replaced

by bus 96. The conversion of this tortuous route enabled the end of the last few Brill-Maley short wheelbase four-wheelers purchased between 1905-8. Then, after 30 August, the Ladywood tramway service 33 was replaced by the 95 bus route. Standard residents at Rosebery Street became the majority of the Leyland-bodied TD6c buses, 1270-319.

The bus fleet thus remained under great pressure, exacerbated by the exceptionally hard winter of early 1947 and the COG5s already being withdrawn. The last Morris Imperial (544) was not withdrawn until the end of May 1947 when seven unrebodied petrol-engined Regents, all Metro-Cammell-bodied, still survived. Two of these, 488/99, lasted until the end of the year. Seats of withdrawn buses were used to replace the slatted seats in the wartime deliveries.

One hundred and seventy-five new buses had been ordered in 1945; further orders in 1946/7 meant that a total of 785 vehicles were expected but production restrictions were not helping. Relief came at last with the first deliveries of postwar buses. Metro-Cammell-bodied

Daimler CVA6 1481 (GOE 481) was passed for service on 20 June 1947, the first of 75 taking fleet numbers up to 1555 and all allocated to Harborne garage, then stocked with a lot of worn out early COG5s. The new Daimlers had AEC 7.7-litre engines. The destination blinds of postwar buses could be longer, capable of 60 different displays, reducing the number of supplementary radiator boards, sometimes up to six, previously required on some duties. BCT had discovered that the khaki roof applied as wartime camouflage was very practical, disguising dirt, and this was now part of the standard livery. A finalised shade of khaki would be adopted from mid-1948.

A month later the first of 15 RT-type AEC Regents entered service at Acocks Green. The Park Royal bodies of 1631-45 (GOE 631-45) had similar recessed glazing as the CVA6s but there the resemblance ended. London specifications were included, such as four-bay construction and these were the only postwar BCT buses to have winding gear for the opening windows. Birmingham's prewar buses had half-drop ventilators operated by (high-maintenance) winding gear but the postwar half-drops

were lowered by pinch grips which were either hard to lower or would crash wide open to the annoyance of other passengers and then jam in the runners when you attempted to raise them! Birmingham requirements incorporated were lots of polished woodwork inside and, less happily on the RTs, a sloping windscreen.

The glazing style on the CVA6s and RTs was to be overtaken by a flusher style, as seen on Brush prototype 1235. The modified style was adopted on Metro-Cammell bodies from 1556 onwards, these being 75 further Daimlers, this time on CVG6 chassis with Gardner 6LW engines, delivered in 1947/8. The delay to vehicle replacement caused by the war had revealed that bodies could last longer if areas such as bulkhead pillars were stronger and this knowledge was employed on the postwar fleet. This added to the weight, hence the choice of the 6LW. The early postwar bodies would prove superb, capable of 20 years with little difficulty. Production was hampered, however, by material shortages that had to be solved by variations to the specification. Lower-saloon moquette is one example, some CVA6s had a non-standard pattern while leathercloth instead of moquette was fitted to the sides and seatbacks of many CVG6s. Nos 1556-85 were allocated to Selly Oak (replacing early COG5s) and 1586-1630 to Perry Barr.

The rate of COG5 withdrawals increased markedly and some were converted to departmental vehicles, replacing 504s and 507s. Nevertheless the backlog of overhauls, bringing the condition of the fleet back to the quality required by BCT, was beyond the capacity of Tyburn Road Works. With tramway replacement also in mind, the overhaul programme was boosted from November 1947 as some buses with a reasonable expectancy of life were sent to Samlesbury Engineering Ltd in Lancashire for refurbishment. The bodies, all Metro-Cammell, were stripped and lower-body parts and frames renewed where necessary, reassembled and fully repainted ready for service. COG5s dating from late 1936 and 1937 were initially sent, switching to 1938/9 models after about a year. This brought another round of body exchanges until the programme ceased in July 1949, by which time 110

bodies had been treated. One other body repair job handled by Samlesbury in spring 1948 was accident damaged Duple-bodied Daimler CWA6 1362.

Leyland had established itself as BCT's alternative supplier in the years immediately preceding the war and 235 PD2s and PS2s had been ordered by mid-1947. These would have Leyland's new powerful 9.8-litre engine — the O.600 — and synchromesh gearboxes, as yet not in production on buses. There was no 'easy change' gearbox option but the easier handling characteristics offered by the synchromesh shelved BCT's dislike of manual gearboxes for the time being. Leyland's obvious delight at receiving further orders, including 50 with Leyland's own bodies, prompted the manufacturer to agree to supply almost immediately a pre-production PD2 prototype. The bus was the only postwar bus to reuse an old fleet number — No 296 — carrying on from prewar Leylands 211-95 and was passed for service on 29 September 1947 with registration HOJ 396. It carried Leyland's standard 56-seat bodywork, very neat but including a curved rather than Birmingham's preferred straight staircase. It was joined at Yardley Wood garage in March 1948 by another PD2, 1656 (HOV 656), with a Brush body of generally similar appearance to the Daimlers then being delivered. This was the first of 100 buses of which bulk delivery began in August and extended into 1949. Nos 1656-1705 were all allocated to Yardley Wood and 1706-55 to Perry Barr where, apart from rare slight adjustments between the two garages, they would remain for their long lives. Registrations HOV 656-999 were booked for buses 1656-1999.

One hundred and seventy-five buses comprised the next batch of Metro-Cammell Daimlers and, again, only half had Gardner engines. Nos 1756-1843 were CVD6 models with Daimler's own CD6 engines, which all arrived in 1948, and 1844-1930 were Gardner 6LW-engined CVG6 models, delivery of these extending into 1949. The earlier CVD6s continued to have handrails across the front windows but the standard specification was changed in spring 1948 to have them below the windows, 1627-30/57-755 also being delivered late enough to incorporate this modification. One bus, No 1803, was fitted in July 1949 with separate number blinds, additional at the front and replacing at the side and rear the traditional destination blinds. This arrangement would become standard from 1950 but 1803 always was a head-turner by combining the later displays with exposed radiator. 1756-99 were new to Acocks Green but all would move on before the end of 1950.

The conversion of the Stechford trams along Bordesley Green to buses occurred on 3 October 1948. The replacing bus routes were numbered 53 via Garrison Lane and 54 via Deritend. There were short workings to Belchers Lane, numbered 51 and 52 respectively; these were renumbered 53B and 54B from July 1951. For many years until now, Arthur Street (later known as Coventry Road) depot had operated trams and the Coventry Road trolleybuses. Now the tram element became motorbuses, although the replacements were formally allocated to Liverpool Street that had nominally all of 1800-43 in its care. The trolleybus route also received some attention with an additional turning point being installed, at Wagon Lane, operational from January 1949.

New CVG6s 1844-80 were allocated to Highgate Road, 1881-1900 to Barford Street, and 1901-30 to Liverpool Street.

Daimler CVG6 buses 1624 and 1620 near the end of lives spanning almost 19 years but are still at work on one of the most arduous routes in the city. This is Lea Village where 1620 is terminating; 1624 is travelling the full length of the route to Tile Cross island. They look much as they did when new; the cognoscenti can approximately date photographs by small changes, starting with the removal of the radiator blinds. The straw coloured insert within the herzim mouldings did not survive the introduction of spray painting from 1957/8, being painted black with the mouldings. Slimmer lettering and fleet numbers were introduced in 1960, the side numbers transferring to below the windows and becoming black. Semaphore trafficators were replaced by flashing indicators around the same time. *D. Maxted/MRK Collection*

The clash of BCT and London Transport ideas on body styling put the 15 1947 Park Royal bodies on RT-style AEC Regent III chassis into an architectural class of their own! The crew of 1635, and Leyland 1684 behind, are taking advantage in Bull Street of one of several Fordson mobile canteens owned by BCT. *The Transport Museum, Wythall*

The RT chassis was a superb design to meet the needs of London Transport and incorporated AEC A204 9.6-litre engines, compressed air-operated preselective gearboxes and brakes. Nos 1631-45 were destined to spend their lives at Acocks Green apart from a sojourn for 1643-5 at Barford Street between 1948 and 1950, possibly to give experience of compressed air brakes and gearchanges on the very intensive city services such as the Inner Circle worked by that garage.

Acocks Green garage was well-endowed with Crossleys, the instructors' favourite, so it is surprising to see Regent 1637 on driver tuition. New drivers received familiarisation on all types at a garage, however, including, for Acocks Green personnel, an hour or so on a preselector Regent. *D. Williams/courtesy Graham Harper*

The service vehicle fleet was modernised in 1947/8 with 1934/5 AOG-registered Daimler COG5s whose double-deck bus bodies were worn out. Here former Northern Counties-bodied 674, now numbered 27 in the service vehicle fleet, retrieves failed Leyland PD2 1686 in St Martins Lane, then a backwater behind the church of that name in the Bull Ring but now a major thoroughfare. The police sergeant striding over from nearby Digbeth police station is not a good sign! Most of these conversions would have exceptionally long lives, some surviving into West Midlands PTE years. *MRK Collection*

No 679 was converted to take all that small change collected on the buses to the bank in Colmore Row where it is seen here in November 1961. In these days of high security vans and safety obsessions, how about the chap leaning out of the door left open to give ventilation to the cluster of conductors within, guarding the hoard? *F. W. York/courtesy The Transport Museum, Wythall*

Tyburn Road Works gets the fleet back into shape. Overhauled Daimler COG5 849 is prominent in this view, probably taken in mid-1948. Most of the buses are COG5s but there is a Leyland-bodied TD6c near the back and Metro-Cammell bodied Leyland TD6c 283 on the extreme right. An AEC petrol engine is nearest the camera. *Birmingham City Transport*

Another Tyburn Road Works view from mid-1948. There is no clue as to the COG5 losing its body but, behind, the former body of 1047 is ready for a COG5 chassis to take it to Samlesbury for refurbishment — it would be mounted on 1024. Next to that is the wartime Brush body formerly fitted to AEC Regent 398 and being prepared for transfer to one of the dual-control Regent chassis. *Birmingham City Transport*

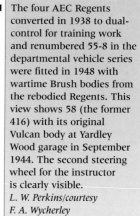

The four AEC Regents converted in 1938 to dual-control for training work and renumbered 55-8 in the departmental vehicle series were fitted in 1948 with wartime Brush bodies from the rebodied Regents. This view shows 58 (the former 416) with its original Vulcan body at Yardley Wood garage in September 1944. The second steering wheel for the instructor is clearly visible.
L. W. Perkins/courtesy F. A. Wycherley

Regent dual-control trainer 55 is seen with its replacement Brush body in November 1948. It is a combination of the chassis of 388 and the second body of 448. *John Edgington*

41

The Leyland Titan PD2 was a new design introducing the O.600 engine and synchromesh gearbox — the latter, although manual, was expected to be the next best thing to a preselector. Prototype PD2 296 is often perceived as the bus that won the postwar orders for Leyland. In fact 100 PD2s had already been ordered off the drawing board in 1946 and the other 100 were already in negotiation when Leyland agreed to calm BCT's nerves and supply No 296 for service testing of the new design. It was passed for service on 29 September 1947. Almost 20 years on, buses are being marshalled for the next day's service at Yardley Wood garage. No 296 is starting a new line, its Leyland body contrasting with the Brush bodies of its compatriots. *D. Maxted/MRK Collection*

The earliest postwar buses had grab rails across the front windows but, from May 1948, they reverted to below the windows. Brush-bodied Leyland PD2 Titan 1656 entered service in March 1948, some five months before the rest of the batch, 1657-1755, and was easily identified by its grab rails. It stands at the terminus in Baldwins Lane, Hall Green, in April 1967, ready for another long cross-city journey to Pheasey estate. *Geoff Kelland/MRK Collection*

The 100 Leyland PD2 Titans with metal-framed Brush bodies arguably had the best bus bodies built by the Loughborough coachbuilder. They may have looked old-fashioned but these were very impressive machines. They were, however, notably cool runners and cab heaters were fitted in the mid-1950s. Leyland PD2/Brush 1731 in May 1967 leads a line of buses trying to cross fast moving inbound traffic in Aldridge Road to access Wellhead Lane, home of Perry Barr garage.
Geoff Kelland/MRK Collection

The Moseley Road/Alcester Road trams terminated at Alcester Lanes End at the King's Arms public house. The needs of those further along Alcester Road South to the Maypole were met by minimum fare bus service 35. This service had started in 1928 as a cross-city route to Erdington (Sutton Road/Chester Road). Initially numbered 17 in both directions, the number 35 was adopted for southbound and south side city shorts from 1936; the north side operation and thus use of the number 17 ceased immediately after the outbreak of World War 2. Two of the tram replacement bus services, 48 and 50, went all the way to the Maypole and service 35 was withdrawn. Yardley Wood's Leyland PD2 Titans, such as 1657 and 1691 here in August 1949, thus would no longer be a familiar sight at the Maypole as Moseley Road garage's postwar stock would be Daimler CVD6s until the Fleetline era. *John Edgington*

The Alcester Lanes End tram terminus on 10 September 1949. Tram 363 is in postwar livery but still has shaded numerals; its motorman and conductress wait for departure time back to the city centre. A bored-looking man stands at the gnarled cast-iron compulsory stop for a 35 to take him to the Maypole. Soon there will be frequent buses provided by services 48 and 50. *A. N. H. Glover/courtesy F. A. Wycherley*

Daimler CVD6 1798 was three months old when seen in October 1948 at the city terminus, then on the downward gradient of Albert Street, of service 44A to Lincoln Road North, Acocks Green. This bus had experimental hinged vents in the front windows that gave it an unfortunate resemblance to the wartime austerity vehicles. Trolleybus 44 loads behind for Sheldon and a Midland Red FEDD just noses into the picture. A tramcar is loading in Martineau Street, a thoroughfare that today has an unmarked vestigial existence as the entrance for the delivery lorries serving the shops around Martineau Square. The distant buildings are in Corporation Street. *John Edgington*

Today we are united in Europe but in 1948 the continent and its road system were in ruins. Only three years previously British servicemen, including many BCT employees, had been battling their way towards Berlin. It was against this background that Daimler despatched six buses to the British Exhibition in Copenhagen, Denmark. Amongst them was Birmingham CVD6 1822. The route was via Germany involving difficult ferry crossings because bridges had been destroyed. The crew reported miles of devastation and people living in cellars and sheds. No 1822 is seen on the return journey at the Belgian frontier post, Adinkerke. *The Transport Museum, Wythall archive*

46

CVD6 1803 was the prototype for the later 'triple indicator' buses. It was the only exposed-radiator bus with separate service number blinds and thus always looked out of place. It is seen unloading in Livery Street, at the side of the old Snow Hill station, in July 1961. *F. W. York/courtesy The Transport Museum, Wythall*

1948 Metro-Cammell-bodied Daimler CVG6 1855 reflects the typically smart condition of a bus belonging to Highgate Road garage as it heads for the city along Stratford Road, Sparkhill, here passing St John's Road. The gap on the destination blind used to show AND ALBERT STREET but this was painted out when the terminus moved to Carrs Lane in October 1948, reverting to Albert Street in March 1952. Guy 2592 is following. *The Transport Museum, Wythall*

The 1844-1930 batch of CVG6s must have been amongst the most hard working in the city, many being allocated to garages working the 8 Inner Circle. For a bit of light relief, they could go round the 19 City Circle, the closest to the centre and least famous of the three circular bus routes around Birmingham. The photographer did well to catch Liverpool Street's 1919 on the 19. By this date, 25 April 1968, the route barely existed with much of its catchment area demolished. *Maurice Collignon*

Several steps forward — one step back

With the withdrawal or revitalisation of the prewar fleet in full swing, the rapid decline of wartime bodywork must have been regarded with dismay — indeed the Park Royal-bodied Leyland TD7, 1327, and Weymann-bodied Guys 1335/7 last ran in 1948.

Towards the end of 1948 the 1929-31 bodies were removed from the four dual-control AEC Regents 55 to 58 (originally 388, 339, 414 and 416). Over the next few months, wartime Brush bodies were transferred from rebodied Regents 448, 391, 401 and 398 which were then scrapped along with the old 'piano front' bodies. By and large, however, the rebodied petrol-engined Regents ran until 1950.

The withdrawal of all wartime Guys and Daimlers began in earnest at the beginning of 1949 and was completed over the next two years. This did not include the 'Johannesburg' COG6s nor the Leyland-bodied TD7s which were well-constructed to peacetime standards. The withdrawal of earlier Leyland-bodied TD4c buses 964-8 late in 1948 was perhaps surprising, although similar-date COG5s also began to be withdrawn by this time. With a 10-year life expectancy for prewar buses, even late model COG5 buses were amongst withdrawals from spring 1949. Many of these were snapped up by independent operators, including 964-8 and the wartime buses.

Despite all these disposals, major overhauls of COG5 and Leyland TD6c buses continued. The float of bodies had been used up by 1948 and now the principle was to make one good bus out of two by transferring bodies. Generally this sought to retain good Metro-Cammell bodies but the 'Manchester' English Electric bodies were also evidently highly thought of. Of the 'Manchester' bodies on COG5 chassis, those fitted to 727/65, 820/42, 918 and 1018 were transferred to 1120, 1269, 1097, 978, 1228 and 1161, while those on 814 and 1133 remained on their existing chassis; all eight would run until at least 1954. Some body swapping occurred between TD6c buses too but the practice generally ceased after August 1949.

Readers paying close attention will have noticed that

fleet Nos 1646-55 had not been used. These were Crossleys ordered in 1945, originally with Brush bodies. When it became clear there would be a long delay in the chassis deliveries, Brush asked to be released from the contract to conserve its limited drawing office capacity and be better able to deal with contracts such as Leylands 1656-1755. After the wartime disputes over the Regent and CWA6 bodies, small wonder BCT ceased to employ Brush. Crossley took over the body contract and reluctantly but wisely agreed to provide them to BCT specification. Nine finally turned up in the summer of 1949; their bodies commendably to BCT standards. One bus, 1647, introduced sliding ventilators to the fleet, a massive improvement that cleaned up the overall design. These nine had synchromesh gearboxes but the tenth, 1655, arrived in September and incorporated Crossley's option of Brockhouse turbo-transmission, providing an interesting comparison with the prewar torque-converter Leylands. It was externally identifiable by a transmission oil reservoir below the front bulkhead window. It also sported a modified radiator shell

The first 10 1949 Crossleys, 1646-55, were initially allocated to Liverpool Street. New 1647 is seen at the terminus of service 15B at Garretts Green island and displays its sliding ventilators and wheeldiscs, both features that would be adopted on post-1950 buses. The drip moulding over the front windows would be abbreviated to the side windows only on this bus and subsequent deliveries with sliding vents. Garretts Green island is still without the mass of the college to be built in the background. The 15B was an east side offshoot of the cross-city Hamstead to Yardley 15/15A but, following development of the Garretts Green area, it was extended in December 1958 further along Garretts Green Lane to Meadway and renumbered 17.
Roy Marshall

with a deeper top section, which became standard. Like elsewhere, the turbo-transmission suffered poor fuel consumption and performance, so Crossley converted the bus to synchromesh in 1951. There were two types of Crossley engine fitted from new. Seven had the established 8.6-litre engine, classified by Crossley for the Birmingham vehicles as HOE7/4B, whilst 1647/9/55 had a modified type, called the 'downdraught' engine, of similar capacity but giving slightly more power and classified HOE7/5B. It was possible to detect the two engine types by ear.

Delivery delays were of great concern. Buses ordered in 1947, to be 1931-2265, had yet to arrive. Nos 1931-2130 would be 200 more Metro-Cammell-bodied Daimler CVD6s. Leyland had been able to offer only 100 more PD2 Titans with relatively early delivery. It could also supply 50 bodies at a very good price that another customer had not yet confirmed, these were ordered to become 2131-80 although the finish would be completely non-standard. Faced with many orders, including 500 bodies for London Transport, Leyland's coachworks could not offer more bodies before 1951. The balance of the order, for 2181-2230, ironically went to Park Royal, London Transport's biggest body supplier, which offered better delivery and price than Brush. Metro-Cammell was also engaged to renew the small single-deck fleet with 35 bodies on Leyland PS2 Tiger chassis (2231-65). Another 360 buses had been ordered in July 1948. There were long delivery dates for Daimlers and Leylands, and high prices demanded by AEC. BCT liked the specification of Gardner engines and preselector gearboxes offered by Guy but the manufacturer was only prepared to build 100 chassis. Crossley, however, could offer complete buses with reasonable delivery dates. The upshot was an order for no less than 260 Crossleys, to be 2266-2525, and 100 Guys with Metro-Cammell bodies, to be 2526-2625.

From the outset, Guy worked with BCT engineers on the design of a concealed front end, with Metro-Cammell involved by September. The latter came up with a full-front design in October but, by December, was back to a concealed-radiator half-cab and producing a mock-up of the upper-deck front. In July 1949 BCT accepted prices for

sliding ventilators as per 1647 and the 'triple indicator' destinations as seen on 1803. Pictures of the largely finalised front end were sent the same month by Guy to BCT which passed copies on to Crossley and Daimler. Both Crossley and Daimler had agreed that their respective final 100 vehicles would have similar front ends, although Metro-Cammell had requested unsuccessfully that the Daimlers (2031-2130) should be unmodified to reduce redesign and maintain deliveries, avoiding the Daimlers having to be built alongside the Guys. Leyland was similarly asked to have concealed fronts on the PS2 Tigers but the manufacturer successfully fended off the idea by warning of severe delays.

The Leylands began to arrive in March 1949, Leyland-bodied 2131-80 appearing very rapidly whilst delivery of Park Royals 2181-2230 spread into 1950. The Leyland bodies bore little concession to Birmingham requirements apart from drivers' signalling windows and layout of half-

▲ Birmingham buses were exceptionally well-finished, particularly in the lower saloon. Visible here are the polished wood window cappings and ceiling trim, Birmingham's own design of moquette on seats and side panels, plenty of brightwork and the straight staircase. Under the staircase is the narrow aperture for the conductor's waybill holder and, at floor level beneath the luggage rack, the hinged flap to the conductor's locker. This is the Metro-Cammell body of Daimler CVD6 1931. *Metro-Cammell*

Around 50 new CVD6s were put on the road on 2 October 1949 when the tramcars along the Moseley Road and Alcester Road were replaced. The series began at No 1931 and the total contract was for 200 buses, all with Metro-Cammell 54-seat bodies. Delivery of the second hundred, 2031-2130, would be delayed and the buses of quite different appearance. Bus 1989 was not a Moseley Road bus, however, and spent much of its life working from Coventry Road garage. Here at the city terminus in Carrs Lane, its driver leans on the litter bin; in his hand is his individual key for the Bundy time recording clock behind him. The 53 service took the 'back' route via Fazeley Street, Great Barr Street and Garrison Lane. Behind is 1794 on the 54 that went via Deritend, Coventry Road and Cattell Road, joining the 53 at the Atlas public house for the run along Bordesley Green towards Stechford. *The Transport Museum, Wythall*

drop ventilators. Even the jolly design of moquette was non-standard. They weighed in at roughly half a ton lighter than a typical BCT bus; thus some of the most powerful buses were the lightest! Although still of 'highbridge' layout, they were of lower overall height than standard and could pass under Dads Lane bridge, allowing the 2 service, then operated by Hockley, to be double-decked. The road was soon lowered and the service (but not the Leylands) transferred to Harborne garage.

The Park Royal bodies employed the manufacturer's standard shell and its centre landing staircase, but had BCT upholstery. The Leyland and Park Royal bodies would stand out from the crowd throughout their long lives. 2181-95 joined 2131-80 at Hockley whilst 2196-2230 went to Rosebery Street; there would be little change in this split until the closure of Rosebery Street caught up the survivors in 1968. Upon receipt of its new Leylands, some of Rosebery Street's prewar Leyland-bodied Leylands passed to Hockley where the slightly older Metro-Cammell-bodied Leylands were already under withdrawal.

All electric traction to go

On 5 July 1949, the Transport Committee accepted a report proposing the replacement of all remaining tramcars, and the trolleybuses too. Tramways were to be progressively abandoned each year until completion in 1953, except in 1951 when the trolleybuses would be replaced. The schedule of routes to be converted bore in mind the condition of tracks, vehicles and overhead on each group of routes. 375 buses would be ordered over the next year or so, which included some to replace older buses and meet additional demand. These would take fleet numbers up to 3000.

The first stage occurred on 2 October 1949 when Moseley Road depot was converted to motorbuses, and new bus routes 48, 49 and 50 replaced the Moseley Road/Alcester Road trams plus the 35 bus route between the city centre and the Maypole. Moseley Road's opening stock comprised new CVD6s 1931-60, and 42 COG5s all dating from 1937.

A splendid new garage was opened at Quinton on 30 October 1949 and took over the 3A, 9, 10 and 34 services, giving relief in particular to Harborne garage. Its opening allocation comprised 26 COG5s new in 1937, 45 CVG6s, some only weeks old, and the four 8ft-wide 'Johannesburg' Daimler COG6s, 1320-3, by now permitted into the city centre, usually on service 9. Selly Oak's share in the 11 Outer Circle was transferred to Harborne, receiving in place from Yardley Wood garage the single-deck routes operated in the Bournville/Northfield area and commencing Selly Oak's association with the bulk of the corporation's single-deck fleet.

Celebrity vehicles withdrawn in 1949 were the quartet with Metro-Cammell top decks removed from Morris Imperials after war damage (TD6c 1281/3, while the COG5 bodies were now on 926/47); four of the 1937 Regents (1034-7), and the solitary Northern Coach Builders-bodied Leyland TD7 (1328). Regent 1038 lingered on until January 1951.

A superb view of buses handling a shift change at the Austin works in Longbridge. Service 18/18A did not normally operate to Longbridge but certain journeys were registered to do so. The demand was a fraction of that required for the main Bristol Road, nevertheless Daimler CVD6 2008 is heading an impressive line of buses from Yardley Wood garage.
1685 Group Collection

Leyland Titan PD2s 2131-80 carried Leyland's own bodywork, much more to the manufacturer's standard than their TD6c predecessors. Curved staircases permitted a capacity of 56 seats. Those in the lower saloon were, as usual, upholstered in moquette as were the body sides but to a non-standard pattern. Spray painting took the fine edge off the Leyland bodies, and the following batch by Park Royal, by spraying over the prominent black glazing rubber of the recessed windows. No 2162 has the company of West Bromwich Corporation Daimler CVG6 178 in Birmingham Street, Dudley, before it turns right to the loading stop in Fisher Street in October 1967. Dudley's present bus station is on the same site but it has been designed to ensure buses do not park or pull away laden on this incline. *Paul Roberts*

The 96 bus was the replacement for the notoriously twisting and hilly 32 tram which had required the retention of short-wheelbase tramcars. After winding its way through the Jewellery Quarter, the 96 covered most of Lodge Road and terminated under the railway bridge in Wellington Street, Winson Green; all-Leyland 2139 is seen at this rather cheerless spot in April 1957. *F. W. York/courtesy The Transport Museum, Wythall*

The 50 Park Royal-bodied Leyland PD2 Titans, 2181-2230, had this splendid, powerful, front profile. Nos 2181-95 lacked the characteristic swoop in the blue band below the destination box. The lower-numbered examples spent most of their lives with the Leyland-bodied batch working from Hockley garage. No 2195 is at the Hamstead terminus of the cross-city service to Whittington Oval, Yardley, in May 1955. The Leyland GB63/1 synchromesh gearboxes initially gave trouble and all 200 PD2s were modified by 1951; they subsequently became superbly reliable and long-lived machines. *R. A. Mills/courtesy The Transport Museum, Wythall*

The balance of the PD2 Titans worked from Rosebery Street garage until its closure in 1968. The driver of 2228 waits for his conductor to 'peg' the Bundy time recording clock at the city terminus in Allport Street in 1966. The street has long disappeared, as has the handsome Matthew Boulton Technical College building in Suffolk Street that forms the backdrop.
Malcolm Keeley

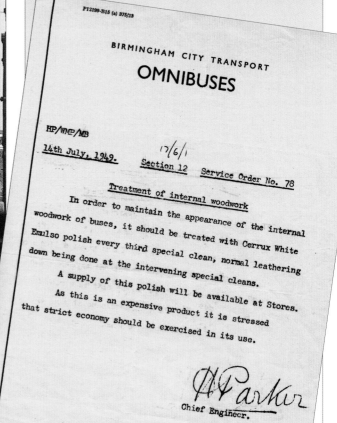

P12199-B15 (a) 375/23

BIRMINGHAM CITY TRANSPORT

OMNIBUSES

HP/WMP/MB

14th July, 1949.   17/6/1   Section 12   Service Order No. 78

Treatment of internal woodwork

In order to maintain the appearance of the internal woodwork of buses, it should be treated with Cerrux White Emulso polish every third special clean, normal leathering down being done at the intervening special cleans.

A supply of this polish will be available at Stores.

As this is an expensive product it is stressed that strict economy should be exercised in its use.

H Parker
Chief Engineer.

6. 1950 — A SIGNIFICANT YEAR

1950 was very much a watershed year in the recovery of the system with lots of new buses replacing the last of the most antiquated stock. The first day of the New Year saw the replacement of trams to Perry Barr and Witton. A new bus service (39) from Martineau Street went via Aston Road and Park Road to Witton. The bus requirement along Newtown Row was met by diverting the Kingstanding side of the 33/34 cross-city service (linked to Quinton) off Loveday Street and Summer Lane, also adopting the former tram terminus in Martineau Street as the main city stop; this latter being omitted by the limited number of journeys operating to and from Quinton. Initially regular short workings, showing 33A, operated to the Boars Head, Aldridge Road, as direct replacements of the trams. A local evening newspaper reported that the conversion had been a complete success. The morning peak travellers had reached town quicker. Both bus and private car drivers found fewer delays as there were no longer tramcars blocking the road whilst passengers alighted or boarded. The Perry Barr terminus, where tramcars had waited for departure time, had long been a particular cause of congestion. Perry Barr received a number of Daimlers for this conversion, including CVD6s 1756-82 from Acocks Green, displaced there by new Crossleys.

The big batch of Crossleys began arriving in November 1949 and all 260 were in service a year later. Half (2266-2395) had HOE7/4B engines but the remainder were able to have the improved 'downdraught' HOE7/5B. The first 160 had exposed radiators and, of these, the second 80 (2346-2425) had sliding ventilators as pioneered by 1647. Nos 2266-84, 2406-25 were new to Liverpool Street, 2285-2305/91-2405 Washwood Heath, 2306-50 Acocks Green, and 2351-90 Perry Barr.

Crossley 2426 was delivered in February 1950 and created an enormous stir in the industry. Its concealed radiator may be regarded as following on Midland Red's coat tails but it was a completely new design which paid better regard to nearside visibility by having a front wing separate to the main assembly. The new design also incorporated both the blue and cream colours most attractively. Despite Guy being most closely involved in its development, Crossley was able to steal the limelight, no doubt having the advantage of being both chassis and bodybuilder. No 2426 first performed on Mr Baker's own 1A route to Acocks Green and 2466-80 were also initially at that garage but 2426-80 basically settled at Liverpool Street. The remaining Crossleys, 2481-2525, went to Harborne.

The next order to commence delivery was the first of the new single-deck fleet, 2231 arriving in June. This order for 35 Leyland PS2 Tigers had been subjected to some change in August 1949. The body contract had passed to the Weymann half of the MCW partnership and the last five numerically would be examples of the new Leyland/MCW 'Olympic' chassisless underfloor-engined model. Both types incorporated sliding ventilators and the new destination box arrangements. The Olympic bodies were basically the manufacturers' standard; window cappings were pressed metal, unlike the classy polished wood surrounds still specified by BCT. Like the preceding PD2 Titans, the Tigers and Olympics had Leyland O.600 engines and

▼ Although all the 1905-8 tramcars had been withdrawn, those of the Corporation's earliest trams that had survived the hazards of wartime continued at work until conversion of service 6 to Perry Barr. Air raids had left No 3 as the lowest-numbered tram in the fleet. Bogie cars 1-20 were built in 1904 as open-toppers by the Electric Railway & Tramway Carriage Works Ltd of Preston, later known as the United Electric Car Co Ltd. No 3 is seen on Birchfield Road, Perry Barr, obstructing the progress of Daimler motorbus 1602. This CVG6 entered service on the first day of 1948 from Perry Barr garage, one of a number initially allocated there but moved on after a couple of years. *R. T. Wilson*

synchromesh gearboxes. Olympic 2261 was available from 24 July and all 35 Leylands were in service by November, completely replacing the remaining COG5 single-deckers.

The first of the 100 Guy Arab 'New Look' buses entered service in July 1950. Bodied by Metro-Cammell and powered by Gardner 6LW engines, their preselective gearboxes were unusual among Guys. On the face of it, they should have sounded like CVG6 Daimlers but were quite different, their loud exhausts varying in volume. You hear today's buses fussily hauling themselves away from bus stops, some sounding like street sweeping machines — with these Guys you were in no doubt that here were buses that meant business as they blasted between the buildings along thoroughfares like Colmore Row or stormed the hills of Birmingham. This first 100 were numbered 2526-625 and were allocated to Quinton (2526-65) and Acocks Green garages. Amongst buses bounced out of Acocks Green was front-entrance COG5 No 94, withdrawn at the end of October.

Finally, the first of the long delayed Daimler CVD6 buses, 2031-2130, arrived in September and delivery would extend until July 1951. Again bodied by Metro-

Cammell, they were naturally very similar in appearance to the Guys but reflected the difference in engine length with shorter cabs and compensating longer windows at the rear. Nos 2031-70 went to Moseley Road, 2071-100 to Yardley Wood, and 2101-30 to Perry Barr.

Just as all these new buses of the latest design were arriving at last, sadly General Manager Arthur Chantrey Baker CBE died suddenly on 22 July 1950, at the age of 62. His career in the Transport Department had begun in 1906 as an assistant engineer. In World War 1 he served in the RNAS and the RAF as a technical officer and rose to the rank of major. He became BCT Chief Engineer in 1922 and General Manager upon his father's retirement in 1928. He was well-known in the industry and his writings on its problems were widely read, leading to the conferment of the CBE for his life's work. His replacement was formally appointed with effect from 9 December and was Mr W. H. Smith. His career with the Transport Department had begun as a junior clerk, straight from school in August 1912. Unlike his predecessor, Mr Smith's path had been via the traffic department. He achieved Assistant Traffic Superintendent in 1927, becoming Traffic Superintendent in 1942.

◄◄ Aware that single-deckers to 30ft length would be permitted from 1 June 1950, BCT asked in February if its five Olympics could be built to the new length but Weymann claimed work was too advanced so they remained at 27ft 6in. No 2261, for many years, was the first choice for the Airport service, carrying special route boards on each side until 1963. It is seen here at Elmdon Airport, as it was then known. *Leyland*

◄ The Bristol Road tram conversion in July 1952 enabled one of the replacing bus routes (the 61) to provide a direct link between Allens Cross and the city centre. The 27 was at the same time extended via Northfield to West Heath — thus the 23/23A could be withdrawn and the two troublesome bridges served by one route. The relatively small PS2s were certainly put under pressure when Cadbury's workers started and finished their shifts! No 2258 enjoys the calm before the storm in May 1969. *Malcolm Keeley*

Solid is the word — these exposed-radiator Crossleys weighed in at 8ton 7cwt and 1qtr. This was unfortunate as a HOE7/4B engined test chassis proved unable or reluctant to start on certain hills. Birmingham's engineers were understandably alarmed that 270 buses were on order that were apparently unable to climb some of the city's hills. A modified differential ratio was agreed but the preferred solution was the HOE7/5B engine, unfortunately only made available for the second half of the deliveries. One critical incline was Hill Street where, in June 1966, 2322 is discharging its passengers and the driver is engaging first gear at the foot of the short, sharp gradient up to Victoria Square. *Malcolm Keeley*

1 October 1950 — more tram to bus conversions

The Lozells-Gravelly Hill route, with its works times extension to Fort Dunlop in Holly Lane, was the only inter-suburban service worked by trams. At Lozells the tram crew, of course, simply had to change ends but the replacement buses needed a turning loop which ran from the Villa Road terminus via Soho Hill and Hamstead Road. The Holly Lane buses showed service number 40 but the more familiar Gravelly Hill short workings carried 40A.

There were also new bus services from the city centre from the same date, replacing the tramcars through Washwood Heath and Alum Rock, and taking advantage of the ability of buses to expand into new areas. The conversion also meant that Washwood Heath garage went over to bus-only operation; it already had some as a contribution to the 14 route. The enlarged allocation included a few COG5 and CWA6 survivors but most of the stock was exposed-radiator CVD6s and Crossleys.

The city terminus of the Alum Rock service moved to Corporation Street, near the Old Square as it paralleled the 14 bus service for a rather greater distance than the Washwood Heath route. This new bus route extended beyond Alum Rock into new housing areas, terminating at the junction of Hodge Hill Road and Bucklands End Lane. Journeys travelling the full distance would show 55B, 'short' workings to Alum Rock Road/Belchers Lane showed 55A. Extensions through the growing Shard End estate would follow, the first in December 1951, these buses displaying service 55.

The new 56 bus route through Washwood Heath retained the Martineau Street city terminus and was extended beyond the old tram terminus at the Fox & Goose to the junction of Coleshill Road and Newport Road, Castle Bromwich. Again there were short working letters of which the 56B to the old terminus at the Fox & Goose would be very familiar.

With 'New Look' buses in quantity service by the end of 1950, the engineers could feel they had broken the back of rolling stock replacement. The Perry Barr conversion had

meant the end of the original bogie cars, of which only six had survived wartime air raids, and the splendid ex-CBT bogie cars, 451/2. Occasional withdrawal of trams numbered between 301 and 450 had occurred since 1939 as a consequence of damage or, latterly, defects. However some of 301-400 survived until the Lozells and Washwood Heath changeover which also saw general withdrawal begin of the later bogie cars (512 onwards). Washwood

Heath's air braked cars were transferred to Selly Oak and Cotteridge to replace earlier bogie cars, requiring their bow collectors to be replaced by trolley poles before re-entering service. On the bus side, the remaining petrol-engined AEC Regents (all with wartime bodies) and wartime Guys were eliminated by the end of the year and the last wartime Daimlers were taken off the road at the end of January 1951.

The Outer Circle was a good route to see and ride Crossleys as all the main contributing garages had an allocation. No 2395, new in 1950 and with sliding vents, belonged to Perry Barr and was the last delivered with the HOE7/4B engine. It is passing Sarehole Mill on Cole Bank Road in October 1966; the mill has since been restored and is now the centre of interest in J. R. R. Tolkien who lived around the corner and was inspired by the mill and its surroundings. Leyland PD2/Brush 1726 is in the background.
D. Maxted/MRK Collection

The term 'New Look' originated in 1947 with the voluminous dresses introduced by Paris fashion designer Dior. Those less impressed by the new buses called them 'tin-fronts'. Concern over brakes overheating on 'New Look' buses caused, firstly, the wheeldiscs to be removed and then a programme of shortening front wings began. The latter stretched over many years — indeed some buses were never attended to before the grim reaper caught up with them. Crossley 2471 with long wings thunders along Birchfield Road on peaks only service 25 in June 1969, just north of the junction with Trinity Road and Heathfield Road. Major road works have commenced which would include a massive overpass at this point. *Malcolm Keeley*

Crossley stole the limelight from Guy and Daimler by getting its first 'New Look' bus, 2426, on the road first. It was passed for service in February 1950, several months before its competitors. For a time 2426 was arguably the most famous double-decker in the country, much photographed — not least on Mr Baker's own bus route, the 1/1A, worked by Acocks Green garage. Soon it joined 2427 onwards at Liverpool Street and became just another bus except to those who knew its place in history. Here it has climbed Snow Hill and is being inspected by Harrisons the Opticians' visually-challenged penguin as it turns into Colmore Row, with the buildings of Steelhouse Lane stretching into the distance. The remains of a footstep provided only on this bus beneath the nearside front wing are clearly visible. The picture predates the Coronation of Queen Elizabeth II in June 1953 because 2426 lacks the small mounting bracket provided for the little flags beneath the front destination box. Its fleeting fame did nothing to revive Crossley's fortunes as a chassis manufacturer but the company continued to do well as a coachbuilder, including 250 more bodies on Daimler chassis for Birmingham City Transport, much to Metro-Cammell's annoyance. *N. H. Stone/courtesy G. H. Stone*

The rear and side of 'New Look' buses had service numbers only. Orange directional arrows either side of the registration number confirmed the side semaphore trafficators; these were later converted to orange circles, generally when flashing side trafficators replaced the semaphores. The large fleet numbers formerly on the rear were replaced by this size when BCT began to permit advertising on buses from 1953. No 2463 is at Hamstead terminus in August 1962 when the colliery was still evident; the aerial cable line carried buckets of spoil. *F. W. York/The Transport Museum, Wythall*

Alongside the 'New Look' Crossleys and Guys came the long-delayed Daimler CVD6s with Metro-Cammell bodies, 2031-2130. A royal visit in May 1957 has caused 2102 to divert via Newhall Street seen here and Bennetts Hill, instead of its normal route through Victoria Square, to access New Street on the cross-city route from Portland Road to Perry Common. *F. W. York/The Transport Museum, Wythall*

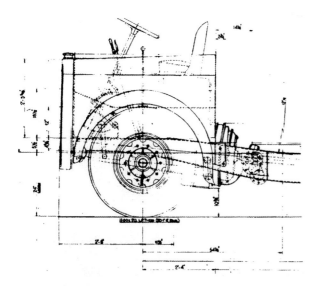

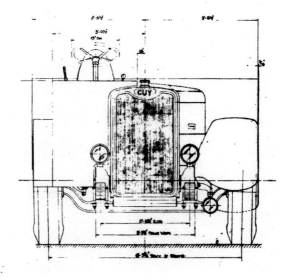

Guy was evidently aware that BCT wanted something better than the rather untidy front end of the Arab III, especially the snout arrangement when a Gardner 6LW was fitted. The mid-1948 tender for the 100 proposed chassis was accompanied by detailed drawings of which these are a couple. The low front dash neatly lined up with the rear of the radiator, which would be chromed, and a new design of wings provided. The gestation process for the Arab IV had clearly begun, indeed the axle drawings were styled Mark IV. Guy soon discovered that BCT envisaged a more radical front end. No 2526-2625 were basically Arab IVs but built to the length of 26ft, the maximum permitted until mid-1950.

Roll over, Beethoven. The Guys were noisy; a well-driven Guy pushed hard to make up lost time was pure rock 'n' roll, especially roll on the corners. Their booming exhausts attracted complaints from the public throughout their lives, especially the residential areas around Quinton garage disturbed by early and late journeys. 2603 is rolling down Linden Road, Bournville, in May 1969, its work that day on the Outer Circle finishing at its home garage, Harborne.
Malcolm Keeley

The 2031 batch of CVD6 Daimlers were familiar at Moseley Road, Yardley Wood and Perry Barr garages. They were withdrawn after 15 years and Moseley Road tended to pick up survivors from the other garages. No 2089, previously a long-term resident of Yardley Wood, departs from Suffolk Street terminus in June 1966; the last of this batch would be withdrawn in the autumn. Moseley Road garage closed a few years later and this route passed to Yardley Wood. *Malcolm Keeley*

The big clearout of buses in 1948-50 interested a number of independent operators with capacity to sort out the tired bodies. Harper Brothers of Heath Hayes was a well-known independent based in Heath Hayes, near Cannock. Amongst several BCT buses it purchased were, in 1948, two of the 1937 Leyland TD4c Titans, 964/5 (COX 964/5) with Leyland's own bodies, followed the next year by a third, 967, as a chassis only. The former 964-5 were fitted by Harper Bros with Burlingham single-deck bodies. The original body of 964 was then fitted to 967 while that of 965 replaced the original Duple on this 1942 Guy Arab I chassis, KRE 850. *Peter G. Smith*

SHOEBURYNESS · EAST BEACH
SOUTHEND PIER   SEA FRONT
WESTCLIFF   CHALKWELL STN.
LEIGH   BROADWAY
68

FOP 340

A number of wartime Daimlers passed to the associated fleets of Canvey & District and Benfleet & District. These operators were taken over by Westcliff-on-Sea which in turn was absorbed into Eastern National. The latter sold some of them in 1955 to Southend Corporation which had an urgent need for additional buses. Southend converted most of these to seafront open-top buses in 1959. Daimler CWG5 FOP 340 (originally BCT 1340) was arguably the most interesting of this fascinating bunch. Its Duple body was not used by Southend, being replaced by the Park Royal from FOP 416. It had its Gardner 5LW replaced by an AEC 7.7 to accord with the others, thus effectively becoming a CWA6. The open-toppers ran for many years, outliving many postwar buses; this is the former 1340 in August 1970. Ex-1429 is now preserved in its Southend open-top form at Castle Point Transport Museum, Canvey Island in Essex.
Malcolm Keeley

The Coventry Road trolleybus conversion

The local press reported 30 'New Look fuel-oil' buses (as diesel buses were then often described), which had yet to carry their first passengers, were waiting at the Coventry Road depot to be the nucleus of the fleet replacing the trolleybuses. The police would be on duty on the last night to prevent the vehicles being stripped as all had been sold to a contractor with a view to converting them to: 'fuel-oil buses and shipped to South Africa. There they will be used to transport native workers to the mines'. This never happened, although dealer and breaker W. T. Bird did sell the 1940 bodies of 83 and 90 to Silcox of Pembroke Dock to mount on unused Bristol K6G chassis for service in South Wales rather than South Africa!

The last day of the trolleybuses was 30 June 1951. The replacement 57B/58/60 bus services included a new branch, the 60 diverting at the Wheatsheaf, Sheldon, into the relatively new Cranes Park estate, but the peak only

journeys to Rover in Lode Lane, Solihull, were handed over to Midland Red.

For the first time no prewar buses were involved at the depot being converted; in fact Coventry Road's allocation comprised entirely of Daimler CVD6 vehicles, including 2626-55, the first of a new batch of Metro-Cammell-bodied buses which took fleet numbers up to 2775 by the time delivery was completed in 1952. These buses were built to the newly permitted length of 27ft although, unlike many other operators, BCT thankfully did not take advantage of the additional foot to squeeze rows of extra seats in. It did, however, convert the seat under the stairs from a single to a double on 2661, increasing capacity to 55. This arrangement would become standard from 2776 onwards. The 2626 batch also introduced deeper windows but passengers may have spotted other changes that reflected economy in the specification. There was a reduced number of sliding vents and rather less of the moquette, previously spread generously about the lower saloon, with more use of the drab brown leathercloth in lieu. No 2701 onwards had shallower cushions with slightly longer seatbacks to prevent a gap.

Older CVD6 buses at Coventry Road came from Perry Barr, Moseley Road, Washwood Heath and Yardley Wood garages, being released by the return to service of COG5 buses at those garages. The practice of storing COG5s as new buses were delivered and then reinstating them at traditional COG5 garages, where destination blinds existed for them, became a feature of the conversions to motorbuses.

Nos 2686-2705 entered service at Highgate Road, 2706-35 at Washwood Heath and 2736-55 at Perry Barr. Nos 2656-85 went to Hockley, one of two garages associated with the prewar torque-converter Leylands. All the remaining Leyland-bodied examples became concentrated at Rosebery Street, followed by the oldest TD6c buses, 214/5/7, which had 'Manchester' bodies. Rosebery Street soon received 2756-75 whereupon most of the old Leylands returned to Hockley.

The last of the Daimler CVD6/Metro-Cammell buses in the series 2031-2130 entered service alongside the first of the next batch, 2626-2775. The new series took advantage of revised dimensions and were 27ft instead of 26ft long. The upper and lower-decks were no longer built separately and the windows were deeper. Rosebery Street had around 20 of the batch, always eclipsed by the very distinctive Park Royal-bodied Leylands that made up the bulk of the garage's allocation. The Daimlers were primarily used on the notionally jointly-operated services with Midland Red. The B-prefixes could not be displayed on the first number track so the destination-box-only arrangement seen here on 2767 in June 1968 was how they always operated.
Malcolm Keeley

With the trolleybuses gone, it was easier to reverse the traffic flows in Carrs Lane and Albert Street and this took place on 16 March 1952 with consequent central terminus revisions to many services to the south-east of the city.

Ultimate experience

Miller Street depot had been testing Ultimate ticket machines since January 1950, thus providing the anachronistic sight of these modern machines on tramcars. The Ultimate proved very successful so the rest of the system was converted between February 1952 and July 1954.

Standee single-decker

The introduction of underfloor engines gave rise to further fundamental thoughts on bus design. One of these was the standee single-decker of which BCT tried a demonstration Duple-bodied Daimler Freeline, LRW 377, for two months from 29 March to 29 May 1952. Passengers boarded at the rear, as then usual for a double-decker, paid a seated conductor also at the rear, and alighted at the front under the supervision of the driver. Normal double seats featured at the front and rear but the central seats were singles on both sides, reducing the overall total of seats to 30 but allowing 15 standing passengers along the gangway. A further 15 standees could be accommodated on the rear loading platform. The total of 60 passengers was thus similar to a double-decker seating 54 plus 8 standees. The Freeline carried fleet number 99 in the series used for demonstrators and ran on the 28A route (and short workings) from Station Street to Great Barr via Small Heath. The standee concept found no favour in Birmingham at this time, nor did the Freeline chassis. It was not the only single-deck demonstrator in 1952: Leyland Tiger Cub OTD 301 of more orthodox layout ran for BCT in December.

Training bus fleet modernised

The four dual-control AEC Regent trainers, 55-8, were withdrawn towards the end of 1951. They were replaced by six wartime Guys, renumbered 93 to 98 in the service vehicle fleet. The Guys returned to the road in their new form between December 1951 and January 1953. All the bodies formerly on the Guys were scrapped, four receiving the wartime Brush bodies fitted to the tuition Regents, but the first two back in use, 94/5, received similar bodies from Regents recently withdrawn from passenger service:

93 ex-bus 1401 body ex-Regent 57, originally on 401
94 ex-bus 1434 body ex-Regent 452
95 ex-bus 1384 body ex-Regent 418
96 ex-bus 1396 body ex-Regent 58, originally on 398
97 ex-bus 1433 body ex-Regent 56, originally on 391
98 ex-bus 1383 body ex-Regent 55, originally on 448

▲ Guy dual-control trainer 95, formerly bus 1384, loiters in Yardley Wood garage. At first glance a typical wartime austerity bus, the Brush body was a replacement on an earlier AEC Regent and has a classic Birmingham straight staircase plus other fixtures and fittings from the Regent's original body.
D. Maxted/MRK Collection

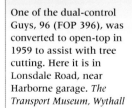

One of the dual-control Guys, 96 (FOP 396), was converted to open-top in 1959 to assist with tree cutting. Here it is in Lonsdale Road, near Harborne garage. *The Transport Museum, Wythall*

▲

◄ An interior view of Guy trainer 93, showing some of the duplicate items available to the instructor. Also to be seen are ventilator and light fittings stripped out of 1929-31 AEC Regents and reused in these wartime Brush bodies. The vehicle is awaiting sale in April 1968, hence the bonnet side dumped on the offside seats.
Malcolm Keeley

Bristol Road and Pershore Road tram conversion

More new buses had been ordered in October 1950, including those for the 1952 tram replacements. By this time, the early postwar bus order crisis had eased. It was already appreciated that the drivers preferred preselector buses and AEC, Crossley, Daimler, Guy and Leyland all offered chassis so equipped although, interestingly, Guy was invited to quote for alternative transmissions. The range of postwar types had confirmed to the engineers that nothing matched Gardner for economy and reliability. If you wanted an order from Birmingham City Transport, you now needed to offer a Gardner 6LW engine and Wilson preselector gearbox. Only Daimler and Guy offered Gardner engines so the orders went to them. Subsequently, in June 1951, drivers' representatives met the General Manager to complain that the postwar Leyland and Crossley buses were more tiring to drive than the prewar buses they were replacing.

Selly Oak's double-deck buses, comprising CVG6s 1556-72 and 1608-18, were transferred away on 30 September 1951 to make room for converting the depot completely to buses. The 20 group of routes was transferred to Harborne which, in turn, passed the Sandon Road 6 service to Quinton.

Selly Oak worked the Bristol Road tram services whilst Cotteridge handled the Pershore Road. Both depots were formally converted to bus operation from 6 July 1952. Motorman of the last tram was Mr William Day who declared that in 33 years of tram driving he had never been stopped by heavy snow or fog (and they had real fog in those days!) The human implications of these conversions is often forgotten but 60-year-old Mr Day, like around 10 per cent of the motormen, was considered too old to be retrained as a bus driver and thus found himself becoming a bus conductor. The first morning was an anxious one as officials and inspectors waited to see how the buses coped with the 8am start at Austin's works at Longbridge. It was reported that the buses had maintained better timekeeping than the trams.

Astonishing though it may seem in the vandal-ridden 21st century, the redundant trams were parked on sections of tramway reservation prior to breaking at Witton or the tram works, Kyotts Lake Road. The newest tramcars, comprising air-braked cars and the two prototypes, 842/3, were withdrawn at this stage, leaving the remaining cars at Miller Street depot for the final tram routes along Aston Road.

The replacing no 45 bus service along Pershore Road extended well beyond the Cotteridge tram terminus to West Heath. The Rednal and Rubery trams were directly replaced by new services 62 and 63 but a third branch was introduced, the 61 turning off at Northfield to Allens Cross Estate. Many more residents now had direct services to the city centre and inter-suburban services in the area could be streamlined and reduced.

The first deliveries from the orders placed in October 1950 only just made it in time for the conversion. The arriving buses were Crossley-bodied Daimler CVG6s 2776-2900 and Metro-Cammell-bodied Guy Arab IVs 2901-3000, all with 55 seats. Selly Oak and Cotteridge's tram replacement buses were all preselector vehicles, either new Daimlers or Guys, or earlier postwar Daimlers transferred

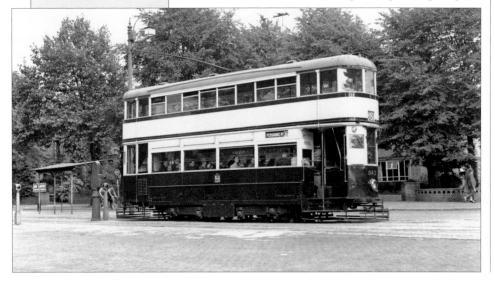

from other garages getting a share of the new stock or reinstated COG5s. Within a year, however, Selly Oak's Daimlers had been exchanged for Crossleys whilst Cotteridge was in for a shock when new Guys 2995-3000 arrived at the end of the year. Astonishingly these six had constant-mesh gearboxes, an echo of the enquiry into alternative transmissions.

Whilst one can speculate that BCT was thinking a decade ahead for replacements for its six dual-control wartime Guys, it is probable that Birmingham was interested in comparing fuel consumption; many operators were reverting to manual gearbox buses at this time as an economy measure. The 1952 Commercial Motor Show displayed several manufacturers' reactions to increasing vehicle weight. Birmingham already had three lightweight buses planned and the first was displayed at the show; No 3001 (LOG 301) was another Guy Arab IV which entered service in November at Acocks Green garage. The body by Saunders-Roe was a creditable copy of standard BCT but the pressed metal interior finish was very different, contributing to the weight saving. The total vehicle was around three quarters of a ton lighter and, to reinforce the point, the original Gardner 6LW 8.4-litre engine was replaced by a 5LW 7-litre in June 1953. Leyland contributed to the experiments by converting TD6c 1298 to a Leyland 'Comet' O.350 engine and preselector gearbox, in which form it re-entered service in January 1952 at Highgate Road garage. It was soon sold to Leyland, continuing its test-bed career with Edinburgh Corporation.

Late delivery meant the allocations of some of 2776-3000 were fluid initially but by mid-1953 they were distributed at Liverpool Street (2776-2807), Yardley Wood (2808-14/34-68), Barford Street (2815-33), Highgate Road (2869-97), Washwood Heath (2898-2900), Selly Oak (2901-20/40-69), Cotteridge (2921-39/95-3000) and Acocks Green (2970-94).

At this time the department was carrying 520 million passengers per year and its reputation within the transport industry could not have been higher.

BCT had used the same artwork for its route map since 1935 and, by the time of the 1952 print, it was getting out-of-date. The trolleybuses had all gone and trams were now restricted to the Aston Road group.

Birmingham used all of the JOJ registrations on buses 2001-2999. The number 0 could not be used so buses 2000 and 3000 were registered JOC 200 and LOG 300. No 3000 was numerically the last of the six constant-mesh gearbox Guys new at the end of 1952 and initially allocated to Cotteridge, as seen here in Navigation Street. They remained there for about 18 months before being transferred to Washwood Heath. They may have been cheaper to purchase and operate compared to a preselector bus but there was a penalty in driver fatigue. *MRK Collection*

The Lickeys — Birmingham's playground. A familiar scene at Rednal terminus for 16 years after the Bristol Road tram replacement was a 29xx Guy Arab IV sitting on the redundant tramlines against a backdrop of the Lickey Hills and the huge shelter that used to throng with Brummies on bank holidays queuing around the tram terminus loop. This is 2954 in 1966. *Graham Harper*

The final tramway conversion

After all the midnight roistering associated with the earlier tram conversions, the Transport Department decided that the final one would take place in the middle of the final day, Saturday 4 July 1953. The trams would quietly slip away around midday as, one by one, they would be exchanged for diesel buses at the Victoria Road stop and the trams driven to Miller Street or Witton depots. It was rumoured that this was to defeat the souvenir hunters stripping the vehicles but the timing allowed hundreds of children to join the crowds out in force along the routes to see the final cars. The demand from VIPs to ride the last car meant two cars ran in tandem. The two motormen were themselves veterans, Frank Bissill and Ernest Worrall having joined the Transport Department in 1914 and 1915, whilst the conductors also had long service.

The official last car was 616 with 'THE END' daubed on each dash. The daubing had been carefully practised earlier on defective car 710; Stan Letts has commented that only an undertaking as thorough as BCT would practise writing graffiti! For the last time tramcars climbed the slight incline up Steelhouse Lane against the one-way flow of all the other traffic. In addition to the official motorman, 616 was piloted by a plethora of VIPs on its final journey but reached Miller Street intact!

Standard bogie cars to survive through to the very end included 31 from the original 512-86 series, new in 1913/4. The newest cars in service were examples from the 702-31 contract of 1925. The closure left Birmingham as apparently the largest city in the world without any form of electrically-driven passenger transport service. One complete tramcar survived although, surprisingly, it was one of the vehicles withdrawn in 1950. This was 395, a four-wheel car built in 1911, to be preserved in the Birmingham Museum of Science and Industry as a gift from the Common Good Trust. A press report implied that 395 would run on rails in the museum yard but, sadly, this was not to be and the tram has remained defiantly static and is now displayed at Thinktank, Birmingham.

New bus services 64, 65 and 66, to Erdington,

Short Heath and Pype Hayes, were direct replacements of the tram routes. Further batches of Guy Arab IV and Daimler CVG6 buses had commenced in time for the conversion, delivery of these would take until the autumn of 1954. The Guy order was 3003-3102 (MOF 3-102), again Metro-Cammell-bodied, and the Daimlers with Crossley bodies would be 3103-3227 (MOF 103-227). Of these, 3009-33 and 3104-28 were allocated to Miller Street, these 50 were accompanied by 50 Crossleys received from Liverpool Street and Washwood Heath, two of the garages which gained some COG5s from reserve, although the latter also got some new buses.

By April 1954, Guys 3003-8/34-58 were settled at Washwood Heath — by now an all preselect garage — while 3059-82 were at Quinton. Daimlers 3129-30 were at Miller Street, 3131-46 at Acocks Green, 3147-76 at Hockley, soon to be joined by 3177-8. The last Leyland TD6c buses had been withdrawn at the end of February, mostly from Hockley but a few at Rosebery Street were replaced by Leyland PD2/Park Royals transferred from Hockley.

◄◄ The 1952 Guy Arab IV with lightweight Saunders-Roe bodywork, 3001, rolls down the gradient of New Street while working the 31 service from Acocks Green garage one Saturday in June 1969. *Malcolm Keeley*

▲ The curiously-styled rear of 3002, the one-off lightweight Metro-Cammell-bodied Daimler CLG5, delivered in 1954. It is loading in Moseley Village en route for Acocks Green in September 1958. *F. W. York/courtesy The Transport Museum, Wythall*

BCT agreed to a suggestion from Crossley that one of its bodies should be lightweight as far back as July 1951. It would be three years before the bus appeared on Daimler CVG6 No 3103. It had an aluminium alloy body instead of a steel frame, saving 20 per cent of the body weight but only 7 per cent of the complete vehicle when fully laden. The double deflector vents on the front upper-deck windows were combined with pivoted vents on the back side windows to extract stale air, and hinted at BMMO D7 practice. That experiment included blocking off the vents in the roof and upper-saloon bulkhead. This 1966 view shows 3103 in Cole Bank Road. *E. N. Pounder*

The final Daimler CVG6 and Guy Arab IV buses of 1953/4 were similar to their predecessors delivered a year earlier but the MOF registrations made a change! Daimler 3177 is just leaving the terminus at the Baldwin, Hall Green, circling the island that will allow it to retrace its way along Baldwins Lane on a cross-city journey to Pheasey estate in July 1968. *Malcolm Keeley*

The story goes that a driver at Washwood Heath complained to the management about the lack of buses with 'real' gearboxes at his garage following displacement of its Crossleys in 1953 by preselector buses. In May 1954, Washwood Heath received the first ten Crossleys, 1646-55, from Liverpool Street in exchange for CVD6s. Then in June, the six constant-mesh Guys, 2995-3000, arrived there from Cotteridge in exchange for preselector Guys. I can't imagine how unpopular that Washwood Heath driver must have become!

Guy 3092 received some press coverage in March 1954 as the 1,000th postwar BCT bus to be bodied by Metro-Cammell, being also the 1,830th body built for the Corporation since the first one in 1930. This was virtually the end of the line for the time being as the fleet had been completely renewed since the war.

There was still one surprise to come from Metro-Cammell which had been engaged to construct one of the experimental lightweight buses. This bus finally appeared in October 1954. Numbered 3002 (LOG 302), the rather upright body, intriguingly with a sliding cab door, was mounted on a lightweight Daimler CLG5 chassis with the smaller Gardner 5LW engine. It joined the lightweight Guy with Saunders-Roe body, No 3001, at Acocks Green garage. The third lightweight was one of the Crossley-bodied CVG6s 3103. New to Hockley in June 1954, it joined 3001/2 at Acocks Green in November.

October 1954 also saw the entry into service of 3098-

3102 and 3216-27, completing the orders for the postwar fleet. All of 3059-3102 were at Quinton, the last ones replacing the four 'Johannesburg' Daimlers. Nos 3179-3203 had settled at Perry Barr, replacing in the process the last Leyland TD7s. Yardley Wood had the privilege of operating 3204-27. Only 10 prewar buses remained on the strength, Daimler COG5s at Birchfield Road, steadily diminishing to nil by the end of 1955. Birchfield Road was considered an outstation of Perry Barr and, although it had all-day workings, was generally known for operating older buses. In addition to the COG5s, the rest of its allocation now comprised the next oldest buses, CVA6s 1481-1515. Some modernisation occurred in December when 1504-15 were exchanged with 3192-203.

77

8. TICKING OVER

▲ A further new garage opened on 17 April 1955 which would be the last to be constructed. It replaced Barford Street and caused a reallocation of routes between garages. The new garage, at Lea Hall, received the 14 (City to Tile Cross) from Liverpool Street and Washwood Heath, and took a share in the 28 (City-Small Heath-Great Barr, which had been numbered 28A until February). Liverpool Street did not entirely lose ground, however, becoming principal player on Barford Street's former responsibilities — the 8 and 19 Inner and City Circles.

In addition to the route exchanges between garages, there were some interesting stock moves. Perry Barr lost its recently acquired CVA6s with Quinton and Miller Street becoming new operators of this type. Miller Street also gained some more MOF Guys but lost all its CVG6s, 3104-30, to Perry Barr and some of its Crossleys. Washwood

Heath's allocation shrank, losing 26 preselect buses but receiving from Perry Barr eight more Crossleys — the apocryphal driver who complained about easy change gearboxes was probably strung up at this point! Lea Hall's allocation consisted entirely of CVD6 and CVG6 Daimlers but there was immediately an interloper in the form of AEC Regent V/Park Royal demonstrator 88 CMV. Service 14 was considered to be a suitably onerous route to act as test bed for manufacturers' demonstrators competing for the Transport Department's future business.

88 CMV had a synchromesh gearbox which did not suit so, the following year, another AEC Regent V demonstrator arrived, 159 JHX, this one fitted with semi-automatic transmission. Although the same length as 2626 onwards, no less than 65 seated passengers could be accommodated in its Park Royal body, without doubt in rather less comfort than previously. The press reported that, in view of its extra seats, no standing passengers would be allowed.

159 JHX briefly returned in April 1957, this time with automatic transmission. AEC was pressing hard for Birmingham's business and, in February, had sent along 9 JML, developed by and badged as a Crossley, another part of the ACV group. It was a prototype Bridgemaster with AEC AV470 engine, and the first 30ft-long double-decker to operate for BCT. As the model name indicates, it was a lowheight design; the body was built by Crossley and seated 72. The Bridgemaster was only offered with a synchromesh gearbox and the network did not have a low bridge problem so, today, it is not immediately obvious why the bus was purchased later in 1957, becoming 3228 in the fleet. One assumes the department was interested in the low floor as a means of easing entry and exit, and the potential for increasing internal headroom.

Daimler was not to be outdone and dispatched Willowbrook-bodied CVG6 demonstrator SDU 711 to Birmingham for one week in 1957. They followed this up with a 30ft long CVG6-30 demonstrator, VKV 99, as usual put to work on service 14. Its Willowbrook body seated 74

The cab roof of Crossley-badged Bridgemaster 3228 was rather low. The tall driver repairs his fashionable quiff at Tile Cross terminus, probably after damaging it bouncing over the uneven surface in Great Lister Street! It had been painted green with cream band during its demonstration period, prior to purchase.
Peter G. Smith

The 14 service was the normal stamping ground of Bridgemaster 3228 when it felt in the mood to work. A variation of the 14, reusing service number 23, was introduced in February 1967 via East Meadway to get buses to the junction of Tile Cross Road and Shirestone Road, as close as possible to the new Chelmsley Wood estate, being built beyond the Birmingham boundary. Midland Red thus provided the buses into Chelmsley Wood. The 23 was a temporary arrangement while Meadway was improved, permitting the 53 to be extended from Garretts Green Lane to Shirestone Road from November 1967. No 3228 thus only had nine months opportunity to perform on the 23 which it failed to do on this occasion, having demanded fitters' attention in Burney Lane, Alum Rock. The soon-to-be-created West Midlands PTE was not so constrained by boundaries and, after taking over Midland Red's local services, merged the 53 to create the very successful 97 route. *MRK Collection*

and it ran for a month from 23 June to 22 July 1958.

Existing buses also played their part in the development of a new fleet. Guys 2967-70/98-9 received hopper vents in their forward facing windows, the first slider on each side of each deck being replaced by plain glass in lieu. No 2926 was re-equipped throughout with hopper vents as well as a modified staircase in 1956, permitting an increase to 57 seats. AEC 1634, Leyland 2184, and Daimler 2851 in 1957 received semi-automatic gearboxes as offered by their respective manufacturers and a number of buses received disc brakes. Three other Daimler CVG6s were also modified. No 2856 received 8ft-wide axles and appropriately widened wings, and was dispatched from Yardley Wood to Lea Hall for the 14 service in exchange for 1630. No 3189 got a Gardner 6LX engine in 1959 while 3188 received fluorescent lighting in both saloons the following year. The ultimate modernised bus, however, was CVG6 2847.

Received at works with accident damage, 2847 was fitted with platform doors and saloon heaters, returning to the road amongst a fair amount of publicity in 1959.

There were significant route developments to the south-west of the city with effect from 21 July 1957. The 20 group of Weoley Castle services, worked out of Harborne garage, were extensively revised to form new services 21 and 22, with the night service NS20A being renumbered NS22.

More straightforward was a variation of the Pershore Road 45 service, turning off the main road at Camp Lane and introducing buses to the new estate in Turves Green, reaching initially as far as Culmington Road. This new service 41 was extended, from 17 August 1958, via Longbridge Lane to Central Avenue. Cotteridge garage gained, for the initial stage, additional Guys, including some from Selly Oak, partly replaced there by Crossleys gathered from elsewhere.

Willowbrook-bodied Daimler CVG6-30 demonstrator VKV 99 at work on the 14 service. The press made special note of its translucent plastic roof. It was one of only two 30ft-long CVG6s built by Daimler with the Birmingham-style bonnet assembly (the other being Walsall 824), the manufacturer adopting a narrower fibreglass bonnet cowl, evolved to the specification of Manchester Corporation. *D. Williams/courtesy Graham Harper*

A significant alteration to 2926 in 1956 was the replacement of its straight staircase with a steeper one, permitting the total number of seats to increase by two to 57 and accounting for the loss of the small window at the rear of the lower-deck. Visually more distinctive, however, was equipping it throughout with hopper ventilators; the rain deflector above the upper-saloon windows was also removed. Initially operated from Miller Street immediately after modification, it returned to Cotteridge where it ran for many years but, by March 1968, new Daimler Fleetlines had forced it to move to Acocks Green garage. Also evident in this High Street scene is the partial removal of the upper raised belt rail to permit larger advertisements. This modification was carried out to many 1951-4 Metro-Cammell bodies in the 1960s. *Malcolm Keeley*

Two CVG6s, 2799 and 2880, received 'Manchester' fibreglass bonnet cowls. This is 2799 in Station Street in August 1958. In search of economy, BCT evolved its own design of perforated sheet-metal grille, a grim design in use from 1964. *F. W. York/The Transport Museum, Wythall*

No 2969 was one of the Guys selected for trials of front hopper vents. In each case, the first sliding vent on each side on both decks was removed. This was Navigation Street terminus in 1966. *Malcolm Keeley*

9. 1960S: NEW DECADE — NEW ERA

This was a time of major reconstruction in the city centre and consequently many changes to the bus services. A particular loss was Martineau Street, for so long a major terminus of City Transport trams and buses, which closed to traffic in October 1960 and its services transferred to Union Street. It had come into being at the same time as Corporation Street and was named after the then Mayor of Birmingham. The geography of the street pattern changed completely in the rebuilding of this area, although the name lived on in Martineau Square, in the same vicinity.

Trimming of frequencies was now a regular occurrence and it was possible to withdraw all the reinstated Daimler COG5 buses in 1960. BCT was able to loan CVG6s 1559/62/9-75/7-9/87/8/90, 1606/8/12/4/30 to Wolverhampton Corporation during the first five months of 1961; some of them were stored on return and would never run again in BCT service.

The supply of demonstrators from manufacturers anxious to capture orders for the replacement of the early postwar fleet grew in 1960; four being operated from Lea Hall garage. The Transport Committee had decided future buses would have doors but needed to determine the door position. AEC supplied another Bridgemaster, this time with a front-entrance Park Royal body of quite exceptional ugliness. In full BCT livery, 2211 MK's stay began in June and lasted into 1961; it was allocated fleet number 3229 but never carried it. Conductors liked the circulating space it gave and the lessening of responsibility thanks to the doors. However, they preferred buses with the entrance ahead of the front axle as drivers had complete control over loading and the conductor had more time for fare collection. First to this configuration, for one week in July only, was Guy Wulfrunian 8072 DA. The Gardner 6LX engine should have suited BCT but it was fitted between the entrance and the driver — noisy, cramped and too heavy. Next up was Leyland Atlantean 460 MTE which arrived in full livery in September. This was evidently agreeable, being purchased in May 1961 and numbered

3230. Finally, in December, after exhibition at the Commercial Motor Show in BCT livery, came the prototype Daimler Fleetline, 7000 HP. This bus also spurned the opportunity to carry fleet number 3229 and stayed for less than two months before moving on to demonstrate to other operators. The Fleetline had a dropped rear axle and offered real improvements in step heights and headroom. While 7000 HP was displayed with a Daimler engine, the manufacturer was advising that the production Fleetlines would have Gardner engines … now BCT was interested.

BCT thus decided to extend its trials by ordering ten Leyland Atlanteans and ten Daimler Fleetlines, all with Metro-Cammell 72-seat bodies. The Atlanteans arrived first, entering service from Hockley garage on 5 November 1961, primarily on service 96 (City to Winson Green). They were numbered 3231-40 (231-40 DOC). The 10 Daimler Fleetlines, 3241-50 (241-50 DOC), quickly followed, the first entering service in January 1962. The second trial service was the 43, the one-time trolleybus service 7 between the City and Nechells, operated by Liverpool Street garage. Both garages then had some of each type to

87

ensure fair comparisons; 3236-43/9-50 ran from Liverpool Street whilst Hockley operated the remainder, including the ex-demonstrator Atlantean, 3230.

The new arrivals, plus service cuts, enabled the first quantity sale of postwar buses in May 1962. Included in the batch of 50 were many of the oldest buses, the GOE-registered CVA6s and CVG6s, plus the odd HOV that had been accident damaged.

The Fleetline, with its economical and reliable Gardner 6LX engine, quickly established itself as favourite and the manufacturer was rewarded with an order for 300 chassis to be delivered at the rate of 100 over the next three years. Interestingly, the bodies were to be dual-sourced, half each year being bodied by Metro-Cammell and Park Royal, the latter not previously a major supplier to BCT.

Members of the prototype batch of Fleetlines would be loaned not only to garages about to receive the first big batch of production Fleetlines for driver familiarisation but also to Daimler for demonstration work to other operators. Although the Atlantean v Fleetline battle seemed over, it was not until the spring of 1964 that the Atlanteans were concentrated at Hockley and the prototype Fleetlines at Liverpool Street.

General Manager Mr W. H. Smith retired in August 1962 to be replaced by another internal appointment, Chief Engineer Mr W. Goodall-Copestake.

▲ 1960 Weymann-bodied Daimler Fleetline prototype 7000 HP was a demonstrator in full BCT livery for its chassis manufacturer. Here it unloads at the 14 terminus, then just on the city side of Tile Cross island. *The Transport Museum, Wythall*

◄ Not to be outdone, the 1960 demonstrator Leyland Atlantean 460 MTE also initially worked in full livery from Lea Hall on service 14. It was purchased and numbered 3230 the following year while it was briefly working from Rosebery Street. It settled in at Hockley, basically on the 96 service and was soon joined by examples from the trial batches of Atlanteans and Fleetlines, 3231-50. Sundays in particular would see them escape onto other routes, here it is loading in Livery Street, ready to stretch its legs on the run to Dudley in August 1966. *Maurice Collignon*

No 3230 and the 1961 trial batch of Leyland Atlanteans, 3231-40, were all allocated to Hockley from May 1964. They moved to Yardley Wood garage in 1967, in exchange for 35xx Fleetlines modified for one-man-operation on service 96 to Winson Green, the Atlanteans' previous main activity. Route suffix letters could be an additional source of interest. The 37A was a rare short working of the Hall Green to High Street service and operated just once each weekday morning. It commenced at the junction of Stratford Road and Fox Hollies Road; 3233 is about to turn there to take up the journey in June 1969. *Malcolm Keeley*

At first glance the trial batches of Atlanteans and Fleetlines looked identical but the latter had a lower build. Internally, the Atlanteans had filament lights whilst the Fleetlines had fluorescents. There was no chance of mistaking them by ear, either! The ten prototype Fleetlines were concentrated at Liverpool Street from May 1964. This was more than the 43 Nechells service required so, in the autumn, they were exchanged for 3251-6 at Perry Barr and assisted in the conversion of the 33 service to large-capacity buses. This lucky shot shows 3247, 3250 and 3249 climbing Kingstanding Road in July 1969, before widening to dual-carriageway, the grass showing signs of drought. The earlier Fleetlines were not particularly pleasant to ride. The design of engine mountings transmitted vibration throughout the vehicle; later Fleetlines had better resilience.
Malcolm Keeley

The production Fleetlines had a neater arrangement of destination and service numbers all worked from the lower saloon, the full benefit of which would not be appreciated until they were converted to driver-only operation. 1964 deliveries 3351-84 were allocated to Moseley Road garage to convert the 50 to large-capacity buses and, at weekends, they assisted on other services like 3382, here at Moseley Village, in March 1966. *Maurice Collignon*

▲ The Fleetline era begins

The first of the production Fleetlines entered service at Perry Barr for service 39 (City to Witton) in July 1963. The bulk allocations, however, went to Coventry Road garage to convert the routes along that corridor (58/60) to large-capacity buses and to Washwood Heath for the 55 to Shard End. Residents of Kingshurst, an overspill estate just outside the city and served only by Midland Red, had been petitioning Birmingham Transport Committee for some time for an extension of the 55 Shard End route. Not wishing to upset the long-standing 1914 agreement, the best BCT could do was extend service 55 from Hurst Lane terminus along Freasley Road and Longmeadow Crescent, close to the boundary, to a new terminus at Kitsland Road. This extension began on 13 October 1963.

The 100 Fleetlines were 3251-3300 (251 GON etc), bodied by Park Royal, and 3301-50 (301 GON etc) with Metro-Cammell bodies. Each of the new Fleetlines cost nearly £7,000. The technical press took special interest in the larger staircase, designed to give easy and flowing access to the upper saloon. Ongoing maintenance was

minimised by the extensive use of plastic finishes and the front and rear domes were glassfibre with a smooth finish to both sides and colour impregnated to match the bilious (softglow suntone!) yellow Formica interior ceiling panels (designed to disguise tobacco staining but why was it used in the rather dingy lower saloon?) BCT's design of fluorescent tubular lamp covers, first seen on the DOC Fleetlines, became standard. The Park Royals had windows mounted in anodised and polished aluminium pans set in blue Warerite window surrounds. In contrast the Metro-Cammells had painted pressed metal pans that got more stained and grimmer every year. As if this combination was not lively enough, the Vynide seats were red with grey trim. The double jack-knife entrance doors were air-operated while the fixed driver's windscreen required demisters to be fitted. Real luxury items for Brummies were the four saloon heaters per vehicle!

1963 withdrawals concentrated on the 1756-1843 batch of CVD6s which were sold. A number of GOE and HOV CVG6s were taken out of service and relegated to snow ploughs, replacing the last complete COG5s in BCT ownership, although several more remained cut down as service vehicles. Most of the AEC RT types, 1631-45, were withdrawn in 1963 — the last, 1641, lingered into 1964 to achieve the fairly rare distinction of being withdrawn on a 29 February.

The first 'New Look' bus to be withdrawn was Crossley 2437 as a consequence of a serious accident whilst working the Inner Circle on 10 October 1963. It was bowled over by a bus on service 7 from Perry Common at the light-controlled junction of Alma Street and Whitehead Street, being pushed for some yards before overturning. The Crossley was retained for some years as a practice vehicle for engineers righting overturned buses. They got plenty of practice on the early postwar fleet in the 1960s, and one can speculate whether this was due to racing to make up lost time due to congestion, over-confidence caused by the lower centre of gravity of the Fleetlines, or the poor quality of some of the drivers in the 1960s, escaping the sack because of the increasing shortage of platform staff.

These were difficult times for BCT which had been

Representing the early style of Park Royal-bodied Daimler Fleetlines is No 3419 in Pershore Road South, Cotteridge, climbing the hill towards Kings Norton station in June 1969.
Malcolm Keeley

expelled from the Federation of Municipal Transport
Employers in 1954 when it chose to pay higher wages in
an endeavour to compete with the car and engineering
industries in the city. Rates still lagged behind, however,
and shift work meant no regular weekends or bank
holidays off. When the underlying shortage of crews
combined with seasonal absenteeism such as colds,
bronchitis and virus infections, then life got very difficult.
At its worst, no less than 240 buses did not run.
Furthermore, road staff must have been heartily sick of the
traffic congestion, exacerbated by Inner Ring Road
construction. It only needed a vehicle to break down and
the whole traffic system collapsed. The author remembers
more than once spending the best part of an hour with the
bus moving no more than a few yards from its city
boarding stop in perfect weather. Heaven forbid it should
snow because the only realistic option was to walk.

Not surprisingly passengers complained of long gaps and
overcrowding, yet this was not the fault of the Transport
Department. Everything the City fathers did to the road
system was designed to help the car and, lamentably, one
cannot recall any strategy to assist their own bus network.
Rapid transport solutions were rejected because of cost and
cities throughout the world were turning away from 'route
bound' means of transit, said Alderman Watton, Chairman
of the General Purposes Committee, to the City Council.
No doubt it was hoped that the completion of the Inner
Ring Road would solve the problems which, to an extent,
it did although on many routes the problems were merely
transferred to the next bottleneck on the route.

Leyland/Park Royal 2204 was fitted with an experimental
Bristol-Siddeley fully automatic torque-converter
transmission in 1963. As part of the work, the lower saloon
front four seats were replaced by a bench of five rearward

The Leyland Olympics were very suitable for conversion to one-man-operated vehicles. The first of several new feeder services was the 4 that, from 1 December 1963, linked the new Pool Farm estate with the important shopping area of Cotteridge where passengers could catch city-bound and Outer Circle buses. Some of the feeder services eventually evolved into radial services into the city centre. *I. Whitmarsh/ MRK Collection*

facing seats across the front bulkhead, as on 3228 and familiarly seen on Bristol LD Lodekkas. It never entered service in this form, however, and was formally deleted from stock in November 1965.

The first one-man buses (still a correct description at the time for driver-only vehicles) in the city since 1932 were introduced on 1 December 1963 when a new feeder service, numbered 4, was introduced between Cotteridge and the new Pool Farm estate. The buses initially employed were Leyland Olympics 2261-3, suitably converted and transferred to Yardley Wood for the purpose. Midland Red did not then have any one-man buses in Birmingham but this would quickly change. The other two Olympics, 2264-5, would be converted to one-man for another new feeder, the 20 worked from Selly Oak garage, introduced between Northfield and Shenley Lane on 9 May 1965.

The 1964 Fleetlines were 3351-3400 (351 KOV etc) with Metro-Cammell bodies and 3401-50 (401 KOV etc) with Park Royal. 3391-3400 had restyled front ends, moreover 3399-3400 had experimental heating systems and did not enter service until the spring of 1965. 1964 withdrawals concentrated on the 1931-2030 batch of CVD6s, although 2021/7/8 were recertified, permitting them to last until late summer 1966. A few others were loaned and then sold to Wolverhampton Corporation for further service. Other 1964 casualties were the 10 early Crossleys, 1646-55, by then back at Liverpool Street.

A purge on all-day services with A suffixes took place on 29 November 1964. The 5A, 13A and 40A simply lost the suffixes whilst cross-city services 29 and 29A, the only ones showing the same number in both directions, were renumbered 29/30, 90/91 depending on direction. All this was to complete a plan to use the suffixes more logically. 'A' would be a short working to a turning point nearest to the city centre and subsequent letters indicated turning points progressively further along the route.

The third 100 Fleetline double-deckers were due in 1965 but did not start entering service until October. In the meantime 24 Fleetlines, 3451-74 (BON 451C etc), began to

▲ Marshall managed to include curved windscreens on its bodies for the single-deck Fleetlines, 3451-74, before BCT turned against them. These were curious-looking buses but introduced a handsome new front dash design adopted as standard on double-deckers from 3575 onwards. Snow lends Pool Farm estate the appearance of a Soviet bloc town in February 1969 as 3473 carefully heads for Cotteridge. *Maurice Collignon*

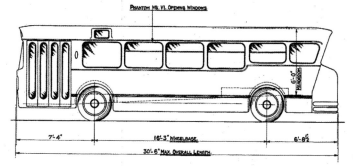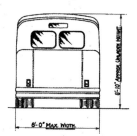

Metro-Cammell-Weymann also bid to build the single-deck bodies but was unsuccessful. Its interpretation incorporated flat screens, 'Manchester' front dash panels and stepped waistrails.

The growing significance of driver-only services was marked by
the introduction of the 46 into the city centre. Marshall-bodied
Fleetline 3469 loads at Queslett, the outer terminus.
Graham Harper

be delivered which were quite exceptional in having Marshall 37-seat single-deck bodies on chassis intended for double-deckers. Although considered extraordinary, it was a merciful stroke of luck that the order was placed before the first generation of rear underfloor single-deckers, such as the disastrous Daimler Roadliner, got a grip. BCT received a number of manufacturers' demonstrators in 1965-6 and did not escape such buses completely, placing an order for 18 AEC Swifts.

The single-deck Fleetlines were clearly intended as replacements for the 15-year-old Leyland PS2 Tigers but, in the event, the introduction of more and more driver-only feeder services meant most PS2s would survive. Indeed 2252 was refurbished as a one-man operated vehicle, including Fleetline seats and yellow ceiling panels. The rebuild was considered sufficiently successful and several more were converted to OMO but without the Fleetline interiors.

The third 100 double-deck Fleetlines on order were 3475-524 (BON 475C etc) with Park Royal bodies and 3525-74 (BON 525C) bodied by Metro-Cammell which were delivered over the winter of 1965-6. The Metro-Cammells had the modernised front ends trialled on 3391-3400. First to be replaced were Crossleys 2403-25 but the 'New Look' Crossleys which followed them and still in service would be overhauled and recertified. Instead the engineers continued to withdraw Daimler CVD6s with 'New Look' 2031-2130 being axed instead.

The last survivors of the first batch of postwar buses, the CVA6s, were withdrawn at the end of July 1966, three weeks before the closure of Birchfield Road garage, which was particularly associated with them. The access had actually moved to Leslie Road in 1960 to permit widening of Birchfield Road itself. The last of the 1556 batch CVG6 buses followed at the end of October, along with the last of the 2031 batch 'New Look' CVD6s.

BCT had ordered more Fleetline double-deckers, the 24 single-deckers meant that the double-deck order for 1966-8 was reduced from 300 to 276. The first of these, 3575, with Metro-Cammell body, entered service on 22 September 1966 at Quinton to be run in before visiting Birmingham's

twin city, Lyon, in October-November. It was a 74-seater but the rest would arrive as 76-seaters which became the standard capacity for rear-engined double-deckers, earlier buses being upseated. No 3575 (FOC 575D) and most of the batch of 38 Metro-Cammells would settle in at Lea Hall for the 14 service. They had a further restyling of the front dash, an attractive design first seen on the Marshall single-deckers. Park Royal at last modernised its design on its 38 Fleetlines, 3613-50 (FOC 613-25D, JOB 626-50E), not only adopting the latest lower-deck front end but trumping it with a restyled front upper-deck! The later Metro-Cammells and all the Park Royals were allocated to Miller Street; most of the latter did not arrive until early 1967. Crossleys 2266-2402 were now the prime candidates for replacement.

New suburban services feeding to existing routes continued to be introduced with driver-only single-deckers. On 15 January 1967 a new route, numbered 46, from Queslett was the first BCT driver-only service to be introduced all the way into the city centre. Single-deck Fleetlines 3466-72 were transferred to Perry Barr for the purpose, meaning more PS2s were returned to the road.

▲ The 1965 Fleetlines introduced a new position for the flashing trafficators where they could not interfere with the driver's view through the rear view mirrors. The double-deckers had an improved design of chassis, known as the Fleetline Mk III. The Park Royal batch, 3475-3524, looked much as before but 3479, seen here in Colmore Row in October 1965, had escaped the eagle eye of BCT's Body Inspector by having the offside lower-deck hopper ventilators incorrectly arranged.
Maurice Collignon

Following the trial of 10 the previous year, all 50 Metro-Cammell bodied Fleetlines of the '1965' batch (some did not enter service until 1966) had modernised front ends with flat V-screens. Fleetline/Metro-Cammell 3558 of Harborne garage stands in Sycamore Road, Bournville Green in May 1969. Cadburys and schools created considerable demands for additional buses in the Bournville area on both the single-deck 27 service and the Outer Circle. Products of the former BMC combine, built at the huge Longbridge factory, occupy the foreground. The Austin A40 (nearest) broke new styling ground in 1959 but was quickly eclipsed by Alec Issigonis' brilliant Mini, a 1960s icon driven by every social class — the three here look like a rehearsal for the Michael Caine classic 'The Italian Job'. *Malcolm Keeley*

Driver-only double-deckers were now legal and, in February 1967, Fleetline 3555 was suitably fitted out. Sunday operation of certain routes into the city centre using driver-only double-deckers began in June 1967 and, the following month, the 96 (City to Winson Green) became totally driver-only seven days a week. Nos 3543-53 were suitably equipped and transferred to Hockley garage, Yardley Wood receiving Atlanteans 3230-40 in lieu.

The 3525-74 batch was the choice for many of the early one-man-operation conversions. Here 3538 is en route for Ladywood in September 1968, on the section of Islington Row shared with the 8 Inner Circle. Metro-Cammell, with this batch, adopted Park Royal's style of interior finish around the windows, employing smart Formica instead of painted pressed metal. Sadly, the change heralded all Metro-Cammell bodies from this batch onwards quickly developing a dreadful amount of rattles. *F. W. York/courtesy The Transport Museum, Wythall*

The 1966 intake was reduced to 76 Fleetlines with Metro-Cammell and Park Royal each supplying 38 bodies. A direct comparison of the restyled front ends, with dash panels all thought to have been produced by Metro-Cammell, is offered by Park Royal-bodied 3632 alongside Metro-Cammell 3611 at Miller Street garage in March 1967. 'Competition' for improvements also occurred inside. The Metro-Cammells had improved interior lights but we would have to wait until the 3731 batch for Park Royal to catch up. *R. B. Norton/ The Transport Museum, Wythall archive*

10. THE LAST YEARS OF BCT: A TIME OF EXPERIMENTS

A considerable number of single-deck demonstrators had been received in 1965/6. This resulted in the flow of Fleetlines being interrupted in 1967 by experiments with new types of single-decker. No 3651-62 (JOL 651E etc) were Ford R192 models with Strachans 'Pacesaver II' 46-seat bodies. These entered service in March and April, and were primarily intended for a new limited stop version of the 63 service between Navigation Street and Rubery, taking advantage of the long stretches of dual-carriageway along the Bristol Road. Twelve Fords were more vehicles than the 99, as the Rubery express was numbered, required and the excess buses were not proving suitable on other routes. Nos 3658-62 thus suffered the ignominy of being replaced after September by reinstated Leyland PS2s. The Fords were stored until April 1968 when a further limited stop, the 98, was introduced between New Street and Kingstanding (Kings Road). The Fords were cheap and cheerful, with manual gearboxes and really intended by their manufacturer as rural buses. Their first fortnight in

Birmingham was disastrous but then they settled down to surprisingly long if noisy lives.

These were followed in September and October by 18 AEC Swifts with dual-door Metro-Cammell bodies. 3663-74 were MP2R models with AEC AH505 127bhp engines and 33ft-long bodies seating 37 plus 30 standing passengers while 3675-80 were 2P2R models with AEC AH691 157bhp engines and 36ft-long bodies also seating 37 but permitting 39 standees. They carried registrations KOX 663-80F and were put to work from Acocks Green garage on the 36 route (Sparkbrook to Stechford), converted to one-man operation and flat fare. In contrast to the Fords, the much more expensive standee Swifts were designed as city buses but were hated by passengers and unreliable too! The Swifts were also used on services 1 and 44 on Sundays from November. In December a few were used in the off-peak on a shoppers' service around the city centre with distressingly poor loadings.

Despite their shortcomings, the incomers highlighted the poor capacity of the 37-seat single-deck Fleetlines. No 3453 was operated as a 30-seater plus 24 standees between August and November 1967, a lasting legacy of this experiment being the extra emergency window on the nearside. Thought would be given subsequently to rebodying them as double-deckers but, in practice, they enjoyed full lives in their original form.

Metro-Cammell's half-share of the hundred 1967 Fleetlines, 3681-3730 (KOX 681F etc), entered service between September and December but the Park Royal 50, 3731-80 (KOX 731F etc), were delayed into the first few months of 1968. Body styling by both manufacturers repeated their 1966 designs but introduced two-step entrances.

Apart from the odd collision-damaged vehicle, the Leyland PD2 Titans had survived until now. The withdrawal of the last exposed-radiator Crossley at the end of September 1967 and the combination of more Fleetlines, the experimental single-deckers and service cuts meant the

All 12 of the Strachans-bodied Fords were initially at Selly Oak, those not required on the 99 Navigation Street to Rubery express were used on other routes. No 3657 is seen in Pineapple Road in April 1968. *Paul Gray*

◀ Surplus Fords were transferred to Perry Barr primarily for the 98 limited stop service. No 3661, partly hidden on Snow Hill Ringway by a signwritten bus stop for its normal job, is working the 46 to Queslett in the summer of 1968. *Graham Harper*

world began to catch up with all three batches. Prototype 296 was withdrawn at the end of October 1967, having recently become the first BCT bus to complete 20 years' continual service without a body change.

1968 saw the withdrawal of the 1844 batch CVG6 buses that had not been relegated to snow plough buses in 1963 and the last, 1857, finished at the end of November, along with the last Brush-bodied PD2s. The last Leyland-bodied PD2s finished the following month. By this time the 'New Look' Crossleys, 2426-2525, were on the way out and inroads began to be made into the 2626 batch of CVD6s. The conversion of the Bristol Road to Fleetlines meant that there were more Guys than could be accommodated at their regular haunts. With Leylands finishing at Hockley and Crossleys retiring at Liverpool Street, BCT contrived to have the oldest Guys transferred to those garages, all of 2526-63 joining Hockley by November 1968 and Liverpool Street amassing 2564-80 by April 1969. The decision to allocate the oldest Guys might have seemed logical if they were to be the first withdrawn. As it was, the plan required a considerable amount of swapping between garages and, due to the sheer number of buses purchased around 1950, these Guys were being overhauled yet again, giving them several more years' life — some actually lasting until 1977!

The AEC Swifts were initially allocated to Acocks Green garage for service 36, the peak requirement for which finished sufficiently early for one Swift to fit in a morning short working on service 32 from Hall Green church to the city centre. It was then the only pay as you enter journey to 'town' along the busy Stratford Road and caused confusion and delays every day as double-crew buses struggled to get around it. An appropriately devilish 666 registration for 3666 as it completes another morning of mischief in New Street on 22 May 1969, immediately before the Swifts' transfer to Selly Oak. *Malcolm Keeley*

The extra length of AEC Swifts 3675-80 involved an additional short window ahead of the centre door, and in the same position on the offside. The last of the batch numerically waits in Richmond Road, the Stechford terminus of service 36, in February 1969. The other terminus was in Sparkbrook, employing over the years varying streets to turn in the vicinity of the junction of Stratford Road and Stoney Lane. This was not always an inter-suburban service, however. Upon its inception in 1936, the 36 commenced in Station Street in the city centre until curtailment in 1958 at Stoney Lane. The 36 had heavy peak requirements to the factories in Tyseley and light off-peak demand. For the transport operator, it thus had all the right attributes for standee buses but the passengers loathed them. *Maurice Collignon*

Short Swift 3670 awaits its next work on the forecourt of Selly Oak garage in 1969; the back end of one of the Strachans-bodied Fords is just visible. *Mike Sutcliffe Collection*

The 3681-3730 batch of Metro-Cammell-bodied Fleetlines were initially associated with Cotteridge garage and its Pershore Road services. No 3729 has branched off the main road into Camp Lane on its way towards Turves Green estate in May 1969. *Malcolm Keeley*

Many of the 3731-80 batch of Park Royal-bodied Fleetlines, delivered in 1968, were sent new to Selly Oak to assist the conversion of the Bristol Road services to large-capacity buses. It was then decided to make the Bristol Road the first big conversion to driver-only operation. Selly Oak would receive new 38xx two-door Fleetlines for this and the 3731 batch became almost entirely concentrated at Coventry Road garage. A temporary escapee was 3764, working from Miller Street at the outer terminus of the ex-Midland Red service from the Scott Arms to the city centre. This is a fine shot of Birmingham suburbia with once-familiar shop names. *Graph Harper*

Park Royal peregrinations

An unexpected and delightful move in March 1968 was the transfer of some of Hockley's Park Royal-bodied PD2s to Yardley Wood. These buses had only ever been allocated to Hockley and Rosebery Street. Then, at the end of June, Rosebery Street garage closed and the B82 etc services renumbered without the B prefix. The 83 and 95 services were transferred to Hockley, along with some PD2s and CVD6s but the 82 passed to Quinton with PD2s 2208-19/21-6/8-9 which looked exceptionally out of place on the rare occasions they escaped from the 82! They did not stay at Quinton for long and, by the end of the year, the survivors had gathered at Yardley Wood and Hockley. The last were withdrawn at the end of January 1969 — but that was not quite the end of their story.

The Leyland Olympics were withdrawn in the spring of 1968. Nos 2261/2 were at Yardley Wood and replaced by single-deck Fleetlines. Nos 2263-5 had been latterly used on another new feeder service 26 (Alum Rock to Bromford Bridge estate) and were replaced by 1965 Fleetlines 3552-4.

MCW had a huge order in hand for London buses and, revealing an eventually terminal contempt for lesser customers, seemed happy for Park Royal to body all 100 of Birmingham's 1968 batch of Fleetlines. These were designed as driver-only vehicles from the outset and had separate entrance and exit doors, reducing seating capacity back to 72. Park Royal, continuing ACV policy of badging

◀ The jointly operated B80-89 group of services lost their Midland Red inspired B-prefixes when Birmingham City Transport closed Rosebery Street garage at the end of June 1968 and transferred its workings to Hockley and Quinton. The latter took on the busy 82 and its 80/81 short workings, initially with Park Royal-bodied PD2s transferred from Rosebery Street but soon replacing these by adding to its native stock of Guys. The author took unreasonable delight in capturing MOF 80 on the 80 in Paradise Street in July 1969. Around two dozen buses had been fitted in 1961-2 with these illuminated offside advertisements. All were 1951-4 Metro-Cammell deep window bodies, mostly on Guy Arab IV chassis but a few on Daimler CVD6s. The advertising space found few takers. *Malcolm Keeley*

▶ No 2232 was one of the Leyland Tigers converted for driver-only operation and is seen on the 27 service at Bournville Green in May 1969, a week before the AEC Swifts were switched to this route. It is about to turn left from Linden Road, shared with the Outer Circle 11, into Woodbrooke Road with a full load of chocolate frog moulders and other Cadbury's employees. The Tigers were seemingly indestructible; after withdrawal several went on loan to Potteries Motor Traction to cover for rather newer designs of bus, and were still there when the PTE took over.
Malcolm Keeley

vehicles oddly to take advantage of Commercial Motor Show space allocations, displayed 3810 at the 1968 show on the Charles H. Roe stand, the bus then being passed for service on 22 October 1968. The remainder of 3781-3880 (NOV 781G etc) began to enter service in order from 1 November.

The earlier ones were employed on a range of minor routes mostly already converted to driver-only but 3813-78, delivered by the spring of 1969, were destined for a much more significant role, the first conversion of a major artery (except the all-night service) to driver-only operation — the Bristol Road services. These had only been converted to Fleetlines the previous year so Selly Oak garage's 37xx buses were cascaded elsewhere. The actual conversion day

was 20 July, just as man first landed on the moon. Unfortunately a fatality had occurred in February when an elderly lady was caught by the centre doors as the bus moved off. A device was fitted which prevented engagement of a gear until the centre doors had been shut for a few seconds. This negated the time benefit of the separate exit.

Four of the standee AEC Swifts had been transferred to Liverpool Street for the 19 City Circle service in October 1968 but the remaining 14 continued to be a much-loathed feature of the 36. Meanwhile the 27 (Kings Heath-West Heath), which had to have single-deckers, still employed a number of the elderly and small Leyland PS2 half-cabs. It was logical for the Swifts to be transferred to the 27

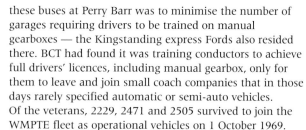

these buses at Perry Barr was to minimise the number of garages requiring drivers to be trained on manual gearboxes — the Kingstanding express Fords also resided there. BCT had found it was training conductors to achieve full drivers' licences, including manual gearbox, only for them to leave and join small coach companies that in those days rarely specified automatic or semi-auto vehicles. Of the veterans, 2229, 2471 and 2505 survived to join the WMPTE fleet as operational vehicles on 1 October 1969.

End of Birmingham City Transport

The Transport Act 1968 required Passenger Transport Authorities and Executives to be set up in the main English conurbations. The West Midlands PTE top brass began on 1 April 1969 although the actual takeover did not take effect until 1 October 1969. All local public transport, road and rail, was to be controlled by the WMPTE but, initially, it only had the municipal buses taken over from Birmingham, Walsall, West Bromwich and Wolverhampton. Not a lot could be achieved in terms of integration until Midland Red's West Midlands services were brought in. Midland Red, however, was owned by the National Bus Company with which the WMPTE needed to reach agreement. In the case of the West Midlands, the NBC decided to sell its subsidiary's local services (in some other areas it came to an operating agreement), presumably to refinance the ailing company and in an unfortunate belief that the Rural Bus Grant would support the rest of Midland Red's territory.

The takeover of Midland Red's West Midlands services occurred in December 1973. WMPTE then had control of all local public transport and could begin to integrate the Midland Red services with the ex-municipal bus routes. Until 1973, the South Division of WMPTE still carried much of the aura of BCT and its vehicles were noticeably smarter than the North Division. National labour difficulties were delaying new bus deliveries, however, whilst the poor state of the ex-Midland Red stock would exacerbate the situation. WMPTE did well to minimise lost mileage but, after 1973, the glory days of BCT were truly gone.

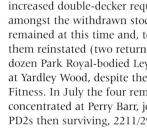

to replace the PS2s. Service cuts meant that many garages had the odd Fleetline working routes scheduled for 'Standards'. Some shuffling permitted the 36 to be converted to one-man double-deck Fleetline with effect from 25 May 1969 when all 18 Swifts moved to Selly Oak garage for the 27 and most PS2s were withdrawn. The increased double-decker requirement meant a trawl amongst the withdrawn stock. Barely any Crossleys remained at this time and, to minimise the number of them reinstated (two returned at Perry Barr), a baker's dozen Park Royal-bodied Leyland PD2s briefly came back at Yardley Wood, despite their shorter Certificates of Fitness. In July the four remaining Crossleys were concentrated at Perry Barr, joined in August by the two PD2s then surviving, 2211/29. The idea of concentrating

The 3781-3880 batch of Fleetlines were the first specifically intended for driver-only operation, their Park Royal bodies featuring a centre staircase and additional exit. Route number boxes were not fitted at the rear. Several existing 'one-man' routes went over to the new buses. 3796 was one of many allocated to Hockley for a variety of relatively short length inner area services where demolition had thinned demand. No 3796 is city-bound in January 1969 on a section of Ladywood Middleway that would disappear into the vast Five Ways traffic island; the temporary bridge behind is over today's underpass, then under construction. Upon withdrawal by WMPTE in 1983, 3796 passed to Birmingham City Council Amenities and Recreation Department. It came into preservation in 2005, one of very few BCT Fleetlines to survive. *Malcolm Keeley*

Hockley's allocation of two-door Fleetlines could escape onto other services, especially on Sundays; here 3787 has made it to Dudley. *Paul Roberts*

The brief return of Park Royal-bodied Leyland Titans to the road was a treat in the final summer of BCT. Yardley Wood searched the stores for suitable destination blinds but it was fortunate that 2223 had been put to work on the 37. This blind was a mistake, soon rectified, as the single line HALL GREEN dates it to pre-1964. Had it been operating from Hall Green to Kingstanding or Pheasey, the crew would have found 29 and 29A instead of 30 and 90! This is Carrs Lane on 2 June 1969. *Malcolm Keeley*

Birmingham City Transport had 100 Daimler Fleetlines on order to the longer length of 33ft and a new style of Park Royal two-door body. The first few arrived before the WMPTE takeover and were used for tuition but did not enter passenger service. The first 23 were allocated to Yardley Wood, primarily for service 18; 3881-95 carried BCT rather than WMPTE blue. Only the first two had the proud Birmingham coats of arms; the remainder had no fleetname but all had WMPTE legal addresses. The penultimate bus delivered in BCT blue was thus 3894, seen alongside 3305 still carrying Birmingham coats of arms, at the 18 terminus at The Valley on 10 October 1969. *Malcolm Keeley*

Buses in Service 31 December 1937

Fleet Nos	Built	Chassis	Body
338-67	1929/30	AEC Regent	Brush
368	1930	AEC Regent	Short
209	1930	AEC Regent	Metro-Cammell
369-87/9/91-404/6-8	1930	AEC Regent	English Electric
409-12/4-26/8-31/3-8/40-1/3	1930	AEC Regent	Vulcan
444-83	1931	AEC Regent	Short
484-503	1931	AEC Regent	Metro-Cammell
81-90	1931	Morris Dictator	Metro-Cammell*
93	1932	AEC Q	LGOC**
77-80	1933	Morris Dictator	Metro-Cammell*
504	1934	Morris Imperial	Brush
505	1934	Morris Imperial	English Electric
506	1934	Morris Imperial	Gloucester RCW
507-53	1933	Morris Imperial	Metro-Cammell
554-63	1933	Daimler CP6	BRCW
208	1934	Guy Arab (6LW)	Metro-Cammell
564-78, 634-73, 744-843	1934-6	Daimler COG5	BRCW
579-633/94-743, 844-963	1934-6	Daimler COG5	Metro-Cammell
674-88	1935	Daimler COG5	Northern Counties
689-93	1935	Daimler COG5	Short
32-61	1935-6	Daimler COG5	Metro-Cammell*
62-76	1935	Daimler COG5	Strachan*
94	1936	Daimler COG5	Metro-Cammell**
964-8	1937	Leyland TD4c	Leyland
969-1033	1937	Daimler COG5	Metro-Cammell
1034-8	1937	AEC Regent	Metro-Cammell
1039-139	1937	Daimler COG5	Metro-Cammell

*single-deck **front entrance double-deck

Summary of Bus Deliveries 1938 to 1969

Fleet Nos	Built	Chassis	Body
102-50	1938	Daimler COG5	Metro-Cammell
151-200	1938	Daimler COG5	BRCW
211-95	1938-9	Leyland TD6c	Metro-Cammell
1140-236	1939	Daimler COG5	Metro-Cammell
1237	1940	Daimler COG5	English Electric
1238	1940	Daimler COG5	Park Royal
1239	1939	Daimler COG5	Brush
1240-69	1939	Daimler COG5	BRCW
1270-1319	1939	Leyland TD6c	Leyland
1320-3	1941-2	Daimler COG6	Metro-Cammell
1324-6/9-31	1942	Leyland TD7	Leyland
1327	1942	Leyland TD7	Park Royal
1328	1942	Leyland TD7	NCB
1332-7	1942	Guy Arab I (5LW)	Weymann
1338-40	1943	Daimler CWG5	Duple
1341-58/66-78/80-4, 1403-6	1943-6		
1359-65, 1426-31/51-3	1943-4	Guy Arab II (5LW)	Weymann
1379/93-1400/7-12/32-50/4-5	1944-5	Daimler CWA6	Duple
1385-92, 1413-9/56-70/5-9	1944	Guy Arab II (5LW)	Park Royal
1401-2	1945-6	Daimler CWA6	Park Royal
1420-5/80	1945	Guy Arab II (5LW)	Strachan
1471-4	1945-6	Daimler CWD6	Park Royal
296	1945	Daimler CWA6	Brush
1481-1555	1947	Leyland PD2	Leyland
1556-1630	1947	Daimler CVA6	Metro-Cammell
1631-45	1947-8	Daimler CVG6	Metro-Cammell
1646-55	1947	AEC Regent III	Park Royal
1656-1755	1949	Crossley DD42/6	Crossley
1756-1843	1948-9	Leyland PD2/1	Brush
1844-1930	1948	Daimler CVD6	Metro-Cammell
1931-2130	1948-9	Daimler CVG6	Metro-Cammell
2131-80	1949-51	Daimler CVD6	Metro-Cammell
2181-230	1949	Leyland PD2/1	Leyland
2231-60	1949-50	Leyland PD2/1	Park Royal
2261-5	1950	Leyland PS2	Weymann*
2266-2525	1950	Leyland HR40	Weymann*
2526-2625	1949-50	Crossley DD42/6	Crossley
2626-2775	1950-1	Guy Arab	Metro-Cammell
2776-2900	1951-2	Daimler CVD6	Metro-Cammell
2901-3000/3-102	1952-3	Daimler CVG6	Crossley
3001	1952-4	Guy Arab IV	Metro-Cammell
3002	1952	Guy Arab IV	Saunders-Roe
3103-3227	1954	Daimler CLG5	Metro-Cammell
3228	1953-4	Daimler CVG6	Crossley
3230-40	1956	ACV Bridgemaster	Crossley
3241-50	1960-1	Leyland PDR1/1	Metro-Cammell
3251-300	1962	Daimler CRG6LX	Metro-Cammell
3301-400	1963	Daimler CRG6LX	Park Royal
3401-450	1963-5	Daimler CRG6LX	Metro-Cammell
3451-74	1964	Daimler CRG6LX	Park Royal
3475-524	1965	Daimler CRG6LX	Marshall*
3525-612	1965	Daimler CRG6LX	Park Royal
3613-50	1965-6	Daimler CRG6LX	Metro-Cammell
3651-62	1966-7	Daimler CRG6LX	Park Royal
3663-80	1967	Ford R192	Strachan*
3681-730	1967	AEC Swift	MCW*
3731-880	1968-9	Daimler CRG6LX	Park Royal

*single-deck

List of Garages and Allocation of Buses at August 1959

This is the disposition of the fleet after the Daimler COG5s had been reinstated for the increased services at Cotteridge and Miller Street garages. All the COG5s, except one, dated from 1936-7. None of them had BRCW bodies, most were bodied by Metro-Cammell. The only later COG5 was 1235 of 1939 which had the postwar prototype Brush body. Two COG5s, 1049 and 1107, had 1939 bodies, distinctive by the lack of the rainstrip over the front upper-saloon windows. Of exceptional interest was that no less than three of the eight 'Manchester' English Electric bodies fitted to COG5s had survived through to this last round; these bodies were now on 814, 978 and 1120. Rosebery Street's trio of COG5s thus had three quite different bodies! All the CVG6s at Miller Street had been transferred from other garages. Many buses would be at a garage for very many years, indeed all of their lives in some cases.

Acocks Green: 915/53/89/92, 1024/6/7/48, 1631-45, 2009-16, 2317-45, 2563-603/14-25, 2970-94, 3001-2, 3103-5

Birchfield Road: 978, 1039/83-4, 1121-2, 1481/3-91, 1503/38-45/7-50, 2017-22, 3118-26/8

Cotteridge: 1556-69/95-1600, 2916-43/62-5, 3004/6/8/34/6/8/40

Coventry Road: 1757-60/8/74-82/93-9, 1815-41, 1973-99, 2626-55/86-9

Harborne: 1482/92-1502/22-37/46/51-5/70-9, 2306-7, 2415-9/79-515, 2800-14, 3059-65

Highgate Road: 1019/30/69/96, 1844-80, 2867-74/8-96

Hockley: 1008-9/32/49/81-2, 1101/3/20, 1763-7/70, 1800-7, 2131-94, 2243/6/8, 2656-85/90-7, 2739-47, 3161-79

Lea Hall: 1580-6, 1601-18/26-9, 1756/61-2/9/71-3/83/9-92, 1808-14/42-3/86-9, 2733/5/7/48-55, 2815-33/56/98-2900, 3228

Liverpool Street: 1881-5/94-1930, 2235/40/59-61/72-4, 2420-64, 2516-25, 2701-16/79-99, 2875-7

Miller Street: 1510-21, 2289-304/88-92, 2465-78, 2776-8, 2897, 3009-33/44/6/8/50/2/4/6/66-9, 3133-60/80-99, 3221-3/5-7

Moseley Road: 1055/60, 1107, 1931-72, 2035-72

Perry Barr: 1050/2/7/72, 1113/5/31, 1699-1755, 2023-34, 2101-30, 2238/41/2/4/66-71, 2360-87/94-6, 3106-17/27/9-32, 3200-5

Quinton: 1504-9/87-94, 1619-25, 2526-62, 2966-9, 3070-3102

Rosebery St: 814, 1134, 1235, 2195-2230, 2758-75

Selly Oak: 1890-3, 2231-4/6-7/9/45/7/9-58/62-5/75-88, 2305/8-16/46-51/97-2414, 2604-13, 2901-15/44-61

Washwood Heath: 1646-55, 1784-8, 2352-9/93, 2698-2700/17-32/4/6/8, 2995-3000/3/5/7/35/7/9/41-3/5/7/9/51/3/5/7

Yardley Wood: 296, 1129, 1630/56-98, 2000-8/73-2100, 2756-7, 2834-55/7-66, 3206-20/4

112

BIRMINGHAM CITY TRANSPORT

CITY TERMINI

TRAMWAYS

OMNIBUSES
ALL NIGHT SERVICES

TRAM ROUTES	TRAM TERMINI	TRAM DEPOTS
OMNIBUS ROUTES	OMNIBUS TERMINI	BUS GARAGES

CORPORATION BUS ROUTES OPERATED BY "MIDLAND RED" OMNIBUS CO.

ALL NIGHT BUS ROUTES   ALL NIGHT BUS TERMINI

ALL NIGHT
BUS SERVICE

*FOR PARTICULARS OF
TIMES FROM CITY &
OUTER TERMINI—*

SEE OVER